COLLEEN HARRINGTON

COMMUNITY RELATIONS

Kendall Hunt
publishing company

Cover image © Shutterstock, Inc. Used under license.

www.kendallhunt.com
Send all inquiries to:
4050 Westmark Drive
Dubuque, IA 52004-1840

Copyright © 2015 by Colleen Harrington

ISBN 978-1-4652-7392-5

Printed in the United States of America

Table of Contents

Community Relations

Chapter	Pages	Title
1	1–10	Exploring Difference
2	11–24	The CJ System: Responsibilities and Expectations
3	25–34	Gender, Sexual Preference, and Identity: The Historical Treatment
4	35–44	The Chronicles of Immigrants
5	45–58	Race/Ethnicity and the Criminal Justice System
6	59–66	Juveniles and the CJ System
7	67–78	Mental Illness and the Criminal Justice System
8	79–86	Social Class: Does it Affect Justice?
9	87–96	Police and the Community: The Significance of this Relationship
10	97–104	Courts and the Community: Behind the Cloak of Justice
11	105–112	Corrections and the Community: Is there a Relationship?
12	113–120	Reverse Discrimination and the Vilification of White Males

Chapter 1

Exploring Difference

"Life is life—whether in a cat, or dog or man. There is no difference there between a cat or a man. The idea of difference is a human conception for man's own advantage."

—*Sri Aurobindo*

Recent events between segments of the criminal justice system and the community have resulted in conflict that continues to increase. Although conflict between the community and the criminal justice system has existed for decades, the current division is one that needs to be addressed in order for the community and the criminal justice system to operate as true partners in the quest for a safe and just society. This text is a direct result of events, conversations, and perspectives that need to be communicated in order to continue the partnership and move forward with greater understanding and potentially change. As my colleagues and I discussed various textbooks for our Community Relations course, we had difficulty finding one that included the perspectives of community members and all segments of the criminal justice system. Certainly, there is a wealth of information about law enforcement and community policing, however, that is one segment, albeit the gatekeepers, of the criminal justice system. This material is intended to further the dialogue concerning difference, the historical treatment of those who have been marginalized in the past and who may continue to be, and the responsibilities and initiatives of each segment of the criminal justice system. It has long been recognized the criminal justice system cannot operate on its own but needs to be in a partnership with the community. Unfortunately most individuals are unaware of the initiatives that law enforcement, the courts, and corrections have created in collaboration with the community for the greater good of society.

It is essential to acknowledge the historical treatment of members of society as previous events and patterns of discrimination contribute to current perspectives of the criminal justice system. It is equally important to acknowledge the role of "difference" in human interactions. Since difference is socially constructed, this affects all aspects of society, perhaps none more so than the community and criminal justice system relationship. The expectations and responsibilities of the criminal justice system continue to evolve with the increase of societal issues that often are not part of the law enforcement

1

aspect but the community service philosophy. The last five decades have resulted in significant change for those dealing with a mental illness. This has increased the number of incidents the criminal justice system has become involved in, sometimes with tragic results. Since crime knows no boundaries and regardless of race, gender, religion, social class, or sexual preference each of us has the potential to be a crime victim, it is imperative for individuals to understand the criminal justice system, the impact on the community, and the numerous initiatives that law enforcement, prosecutors, and corrections have undertaken for the good of society. The material is intended to be a foundation of collective perspectives while allowing for incorporation of current and future events as they relate to this important connection.

Sawabona!

This is a South African greeting that translates to "I see you" which is meant to acknowledge your presence. In essence, it is bringing you into existence by acknowledging that you matter and are valued. This tradition has been established by the northern Natal tribes to recognize our human connection. The response is generally "Sikhona " which acknowledges "I am here."

What is difference?

Have you ever considered how many times a day an individual categorizes, chooses, or identifies difference? When the alarm goes off does someone groan and say "I am not a morning person?" Does an individual choose the clothing they will wear based on their identification as a sports fan, college alma matter, fan of pop culture, as an environmentalist or connection to some other cause? When a new student enters their college on the first day of class, do they approach an employee and identify themselves as a "new student" looking for their classroom? When they begin their class do they introduce themselves by highlighting their differences, whether it is as a new student, where they originated from, or their major? Each of us is comprised of differences, however small, and surrounded by difference throughout our day.

Class activities

Give students three minutes to create a list of how they are different from others. Group students (5–8 members per group) and give them ten minutes to compile an inclusive list. Have each group present their list to the class providing explanations as necessary.

Difference is generally defined as characteristics, traits, or beliefs that are unlike others. This can be an actual or perceived variance. Difference is shared by all humans and can be a powerful strength or destructive force. It is not the difference that is powerful or destructive, it is the meaning that is attached to the difference and actions taken based on the difference that determine whether it is positive or negative.

For the next week, pay close attention to your entertainment activities—how do they promote difference (i.e., academy award winner, nominee, Super Bowl champion, Olympic medalist, all time point leader, etc.).

© Brett Jorgensen/Shutterstock.com

How is difference constructed?

An individual can look at another and identify a difference based on apparent biological factors such as hair and eye color, skin tone, and gender or on superficial differences such as clothing choice, where they live, or what they drive. The differences are socially constructed; however, the perception of those differences determines the impact. For instance, as a society, we choose categories that are used to identify individuals. This is often done to provide a benefit, protection, or privilege for a category of difference. For instance, the U.S. Census collects data every ten years covering categories such as gender, race, age, how many individuals reside in a residence, and whether that residence is owned or rented. This information is used to help determine how and what various community initiatives and services the federal government will fund. In addition, this information is used to ensure equal civil rights and address disparities in services, healthcare, and employment opportunities.

Explore the U.S. census website (http://www.census.gov/#) and discover the variety of differences that matter.

Jane Elliot's Blue eyes brown eyes experiment

Watch this timeless video (55:35 min.) covering an experiment initiated by teacher Jane Elliot after the assassination of Reverend Martin Luther King JR. The young students from the initial experiment revisit the issues approximately fifteen years later.
   http://www.youtube.com/watch?v=-Ggq7XfYl58

© Bloomua/Shutterstock.com

How does the media influence our perception of difference?

CSI effect

   The CSI effect is a direct result of the increase of crime shows where crime scene investigators, detectives, or criminal profilers are able to solve a case quickly, in part due to forensic evidence. Amazingly these individuals walk into a dark crime scene and notice the trace evidence, such as hair or fibers, with their naked eye. While the benefits of forensic science are important, the over emphasis of unrealistic portrayals in the media has biased jurors. This predisposition causes jurors to question investigative procedures and evidence when there is little forensic evidence or to give greater value to the forensic evidence that is presented. Forensic evidence is often considered more definitive than evidence presented by people.

The impact of the CSI effect has led to the modification of *voir dire* and case presentation. Attorneys develop their questions of potential jurors with the CSI effect in mind and in some cases use that predisposition to excuse the juror. In addition, attorneys have modified their case presentation to include appropriate forensic personnel who can explain the processes, whether evidence was obtained or not, in order to meet the expectations of jurors.

> ## Class activities
>
> Watch an episode or clip of an entertainment crime show and have students identify the myths and exaggerations that are demonstrated. Discuss the findings as a class. This can be used as a contest or quiz.

Social media

Social media is described as an Internet-based site that provides individuals with the opportunity to create unique profiles and connect with others. This can be in the form of messaging, sharing stories and comments, blogs, or identifying with individuals who have similar interests. This is a field of rapid change, new sites or methods are introduced frequently as an enhancement or replacement for existing sites.

Social media has been instrumental in the role of communication and sharing of information. Significantly individuals under the age of 25 use social media as a learning tool. Education is greatly enhanced by utilizing social media to develop collaborative learning, increase student involvement, and provide a platform for utilizing various forms of media to augment the learning experience. Social network sites can be beneficial due to the convenience of allowing individuals choosing when they are using media, who they want to respond to and be connected with, and allowing for the quick spread of information within the individual's own schedule.

Personal expression is an important aspect of social media, especially for individuals under the age of 30. Worldwide this is approximately half of the population in the United States and the majority of individuals under the age of 30 are actively involved in social media. Notably college students utilize different sites to share their personal lives and academic work online.

The benefits of social networks are numerous; however, this also creates a new set of challenges for free speech, controversies, or misinformation being shared. Often it is difficult to identify the source of the information leading to doubts about the credibility or to ensure accountability.

An aspect of social networks that can be both positive and negative is the immediate distribution of information to a large audience. When these are more positive aspects such as sharing information about a missing person, a natural disaster, or safety issues, this is not viewed as a problem. When it is misinformation, such as broadcasting about a school shooting and panicking parents when the information is incorrect it has the potential to harm others. When it is misinformation that people accept as accurate there is potential for unrest based upon fabricated information.

A downfall to this may be the dissemination of personal beliefs. A simple click of the button and there is no taking back what was shared. It may be deleted from public view, however, not permanently. Unfortunately, the consequences may be far-reaching. What starts out as a simple complaint can quickly become a legal issue, controversy, or potentially affect future and current employment.

Many employers have social media policies and for aspiring criminal justice professionals, agencies will review this type of information as part of the background check. What looks like a simple prank or good time amongst friends becomes an issue of credibility and judgment. Posting comments about current or previous employers, friends, coworkers, and other professionals you interact with may be perceived differently than intended. Something you believe you've only shared with friends is easily shared with others. Depending up on the comments, they could be considered slander and result in negative consequences.

Try this *(for students)*

Look at these articles concerning social media and law enforcement officers.
Fellow officers are concerned about a detective's vents on Facebook
http://www.lasvegassun.com/news/2015/jan/12/finding-line/

SWAT officer responds to online comments concerning a volatile incident.
http://www.reviewjournal.com/news/las-vegas/ex-swat-officers-file-complaint-against-metro

Flash mob in Miami courtesy of social media
http://www.cbsnews.com/news/motorcycle-atv-riders-flood-miami-highway-on-martin-luther-king-jr-day/

Review Questions

1. *Sawabona* is an African greeting that means "___ _____ _____".

2. What is the CSI effect?

3. In the brown eyes/blue eyes experiment video, the instructor had the "underclass" wear_____.

4. In the brown eyes/blue eyes experiment video, the assassination of _____ _____ _____ prompted the instructor to begin this experiment.

5. Difference is _____ constructed.

6. During the brown eyes/blue eyes experiment video, the test scores of the students who were "on the bottom" changed, how?

7. Which is more important, biological differences or social interactions?

Critical Thinking Questions

1. Why does difference matter?

2. The U.S. Census collects demographic information. How is this beneficial to groups that have traditionally been discriminated against?

3. If difference does not matter, why do job applications request certain demographic information be volunteered? How is this information used?

4. Difference can be positive or negative, identify how difference benefits society and how it can be harmful.

Chapter 2

The CJ System: Responsibilities and Expectations

"Expectations are just premeditated resentments."

—*Jamie Dantis*

What is justice?

Is it justice if someone is convicted of a crime? Is it justice if somebody is exonerated? Or is justice the equivalent of *lex talionis*, "an eye for an eye"? The expectation of justice is that when someone does wrong, they will receive a punishment that is equal to the wrong. Justice is a process, not a result. The outcome of the judicial process is seldom a true equivalent of the wrong.

The judicial process

The judicial process is essentially due process. Regardless of evidence, innocence, or guilt anyone accused of a crime is entitled to a fair trial, to be judged by a jury of their peers and presided over by a competent judge according to Article III of the Constitution of the United States. When society does not agree with the result of the judicial process this creates conflict. Some individuals consider this evidence of a bias, whether race, gender, age, social class, or wealth. This contributes to lack of trust for the criminal justice system. Disrespect of law enforcement, courts, and corrections is often evident. For some individuals, these events and controversies lead to a sense of hopelessness, a belief that the criminal justice system is against them or they will never get a fair chance.

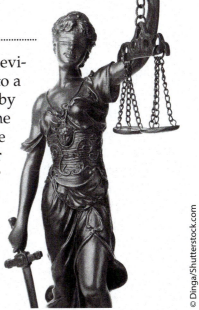

© Dinga/Shutterstock.com

Got questions? *(for students)*

Examine the Constitution and amendments in their original form at http://www.archives.gov/exhibits/charters/constitution_transcript.html
Consider the exact wording of each amendment versus the key points most students are familiar with.

© Myvector/Shutterstock.com

Responsibilities versus expectations

The foundation for society in the United States is the concept of a social contract. John Locke (1632–1704), an English philosopher, outlined the basis of the social contract in his political theory work "Two Treaties of Government" (1690). This ground-breaking concept recognized government as an agreement formed by society covering natural rights and societal expectations for maintaining those rights. The elements of the social contract include specific rights, duties, powers, and the restriction of liberties. This benefits society by providing a collective understanding of accepted behaviors, natural rights, the defense of those rights when needed, and the removal of those in power when society no longer consents to their leadership. The theories of John Locke influenced those who initiated the American Revolution and the Declaration of Independence.

Try this *(for students)*

Learn more about John Locke and other philosophers who helped lay the foundation for the U.S. Constitution (http://www.history.com/topics/john-locke).

The pooling of rights and duties that make us accountable to each other in a larger society provides the framework for government. The structure allows society to delegate authority to individuals to represent the common interests. Through this representation laws, procedures, taxes, and protection are provided. These perspectives influenced the development of the U.S. Constitution. The violation of the social contract results in sanctions which can range from minor punishments to the killing of the offender. In essence when an individual violates the social contract, it is the duty of society to defend the rights of everyone regardless of whether they were directly involved. These rights include natural (life and not to be physically injured or tortured), societal (property rights and due process), and state/government (fair representation and citizenship).

The criminal justice system is based off of the U.S. Constitution. The "privileges" and "immunities" are outlined in sections of the Constitution. Section seven of the Constitution outlines the methods for a Bill to become a law. Section eight includes powers related to enforcing laws, punishments, naturalization, and tribunals. During the process of approving the Constitution concerns about the violation of civil rights became evident. The solution to this was to incorporate amendments to identify protections for individual citizens. Ten of these proposed amendments were adopted and became known as the Bill of Rights.

The First Amendment

"Congress shall make no law respecting an establishment of religion, or prohibiting the free exercise thereof; or abridging the freedom of speech, or of the press; or the right of the people peaceably to assemble, and to petition the Government for a redress of grievances."

The First Amendment outlines the freedom of religion, speech, and peaceful assembly. This provides individuals the freedom to choose whether or not to follow any religion and to exercise their religious beliefs. The freedom of speech is intended to allow for the exchange of ideas regardless of popularity. This includes written and spoken communications, photographs, films, and art.

There are exceptions to this as the U.S. Supreme Court has determined there are limitations to free speech. Some of the exceptions include all statements that injure a person or their reputation, fighting words, obscenity, and most importantly words that incite violence or present a clear danger. A most common example is yelling fire in a crowded building, inciting panic when there is not a fire. In addition the location, time, and manner of free speech may be regulated.

This leads to some confusion for individuals who believe they are entitled to protest anywhere, anytime, and in any fashion. Governments have the right to require individuals to obtain a permit when holding an assembly in public. Private properties have the opportunity to limit what occurs within those boundaries. Peaceful assembly and protest is valued not only by our forefathers but by many citizens.

This has unfortunately become an issue between law enforcement/government and the community when there is a lack of understanding about these rights or when individuals with less than honorable intentions commit acts of violence, disruption, or crimes under the guise of a protest. An example of this occurred in 2013 on the Las Vegas Strip (NV) when members of the Culinary Union Local 226 protested against the Cosmopolitan Hotel and Casino. Approximately 2,000 individuals carried signs and chanted in hopes of forcing the Cosmopolitan to complete contract negotiations, which had been stalled for years. This exercise of freedom was peaceful; however, when approximately 100 protestors sat in the roadway, blocking traffic and movement, this became a criminal matter. When these individuals refused to disperse, law enforcement officers had to move in, and asked, or forcefully moved these protesters out of the street.

In contrast in Ferguson, Missouri, a grand jury had been hearing testimony about the August 2014 incident where Officer Darren Wilson shot unarmed robbery suspect Michael Brown. On November 24, 2014 in Ferguson, St. Louis County prosecutor Robert McCulloch announced the grand jury had returned a "no bill" after hearing testimony in the case. Although the parents of Michael Brown had asked the gathered protesters to remain peaceful, Brown's stepfather, Louis Head said "Burn this bitch down!," to the crowd. In less than four hours, the rioters had overwhelmed the peaceful protesters, burned down at least a dozen buildings, set fire to and destroyed two police cars, burned other vehicles, engaged in looting, vandalism, and several individuals were shooting guns in the vicinity. The use of firearms prompted the Federal Aviation Administration to issue a flight restriction over Ferguson. Numerous fires were set; however, firefighters had difficulty accessing all of them due to gunfire in the vicinity of the fires. In addition, protesters shut down Interstate 44, a major transportation route.

Look at this short video clip (2:36) covering the protests in Ferguson, Missouri, on November 25, 2014.
http://www.cnn.com/videos/bestoftv/2014/11/25/orig-raw-scenes-from-ferguson-npr.cnn

Discuss the actions of the peaceful protesters, violent protesters, and law enforcement. What actions contributed to a further divide between the community and the criminal justice system? What are society's expectations for free speech and peaceful protest? What misconceptions exist in society about this protection?

The Second Amendment

"A well regulated Militia, being necessary to the security of a free State, the right of the people to keep and bear Arms, shall not be infringed."

Initially the right to "Bear Arms" (own firearms) applied to the militia. Throughout time, various courts have applied this right to individuals; however, the courts have allowed some limitations by the government. These restrictions generally applied to those who own, sell or manufacture firearms and included mandatory background checks, waiting periods, and limitations on certain assault type weapons. Although Supreme Court rulings and the Fourteenth Amendment ensure states may not infringe on the Bill of Rights, it is not applied to the Second Amendment. The federal government is limited by the Second Amendment; however, states have greater leeway, leading to varying firearm related laws in each state.

Discussion—What misconceptions exist in society about this amendment and limitations on firearms?

The Fourth Amendment

"The right of the peo]ple to be secure in their persons, houses, papers, and effects, against unreasonable searches and seizures, shall not be violated, and no Warrants shall issue, but upon probable cause, supported by Oath or affirmation, and particularly describing the place to be searched, and the persons or things to be seized."

A search can be wide-ranging such as a frisk of the outer clothing to the more invasive such as retrieving blood or an object, such as a bullet, from inside a human being. Law enforcement, an arm of the government, is able to seize an item when it is considered evidence related to crime.

Often there is a lack of understanding about the elements necessary to conduct a frisk or a search. This creates ongoing conflict between law enforcement and individuals who do not comprehend the legal elements that allow for these frisks and searches.

An officer is required to articulate probable cause or reasonable suspicion to criminal justice personnel. For instance, if an officer has established probable cause to search an individual, it is likely this individual may not agree with this or understand it. The officer is not obligated to ensure the individual comprehends this yet is required to articulate it in a report, to a supervisor, attorney, or judge. If a judge determines it was an unlawful search or seizure, then evidence obtained from a search or seizure, unless covered under an exception, would be inadmissible.

© Kaerdan/Shutterstock.com

The Fifth Amendment

"No person shall be held to answer for a capital, or otherwise infamous crime, unless on a presentment or indictment of a Grand Jury, except in cases arising in the land or naval forces, or in the Militia, when in actual service in time of War or public danger; nor shall any person be subject for the same offence to be twice put in jeopardy of life or limb; nor shall be compelled in any criminal case to be a witness against himself, nor be deprived of life, liberty, or property, without due process of law; nor shall private property be taken for public use, without just compensation."

The grand jury is an opportunity for a group of individuals to hear evidence and testimony to determine if there is sufficient evidence to indict or file charges against an individual. Those selected to serve on the jury are chosen from individuals who are eligible to serve on a jury; however, they serve for a longer period of time in here, multiple cases as opposed to serving for one case.

The grand jury serves as a check and balance within the criminal justice system when it is used. It is beneficial to prosecutors for several reasons. If the prosecutor does not believe charges are warranted; however, it is a controversial case, it may be best to allow a grand jury to make that decision. If a case is weak and the grand jury issues a "no bill" (does not indict), then the prosecutor has the opportunity to seek more evidence before charging an individual with a crime. The grand jury protection has not been applied to all of the states.

The checks and balances to keep the government from having too much power also includes "double jeopardy." This means that once an individual has been acquitted or convicted of a charge they cannot be tried again for the same criminal act. This also provides for one punishment for the crime as opposed to punishing an individual multiple times for the same crime. In these instances, the government has only one opportunity to try the case. There is often confusion when a jury is "hung" meaning they are deadlocked and cannot agree in cases of a mistrial. In these instances, the prosecutor can try the case again.

The protection against self-incrimination is one of the most often misunderstood rights. The right to remain silent or "take the fifth" is another check and balance that forces the criminal justice system to uncover evidence of a crime/guilt without forcing the individual to reveal details, through verbal, nonverbal, or written communication, that would provide evidence of their guilt. The individual accused of a crime does not have to appear on the witness stand and defend themselves; they have the right remain silent, and this cannot be used as evidence of their guilt.

Entertainment and news media have helped perpetuate myths surrounding the Fifth Amendment and the reading of Miranda rights. Often in a television show or movie a police officer will read the Miranda rights as the individual is being arrested or placed into a police car. This leads individuals to believe if they have not been read their Miranda rights, law enforcement has violated their Fifth Amendment rights and anything they say cannot be used against them.

Miranda rights apply to an individual that is in custody and being interrogated about their criminal involvement. Answering questions about your name, date of birth, and address is often part of the investigative and booking process. Those questions are not incriminating. In addition, if an individual makes incriminating statements to a third-party, in writing, or voluntarily to the officer, these are not protected.

Class activities

Discussion—What are society's expectations for this? What misconceptions exist in society about Miranda rights and grand juries?

© Thomas Heden/Shutterstock.com

The Sixth Amendment

"In all criminal prosecutions, the accused shall enjoy the right to a speedy and public trial, by an impartial jury of the State and district wherein the crime shall have been committed, which district shall have been previously ascertained by law, and to be informed of the nature and cause of the accusation; to be confronted with the witnesses against him; to have compulsory process for obtaining witnesses in his favor, and to have the Assistance of Counsel for his defence."

The right to an impartial jury of peers in a trial is intended to provide the defendant with a group of individuals from their community to weigh the evidence and determine guilt. These individuals are questioned by both prosecutors and defense attorneys, before being selected to serve on the jury, to ensure they are not biased in the case and have not made a decision concerning the case before any evidence is presented. Often individuals challenge the concept of peers when the jurors differ from them. For high profile cases, the trial may be moved to a different venue to allow for a jury pool that is unaware of the case

A speedy trial is extremely important to the defendant in many cases. This prevents the government from continuing the case indefinitely. There are advantages and disadvantages to waiving their right to a speedy trial (a right only the defendant can waive). An advantage to waiving this right and allowing the case to be continued is the potential for evidence to be lost, witnesses to forget details, move, die, or lose credibility.

In addition, some defendants may be offered a plea to a lesser charge in order to settle the case. A disadvantage in waiving the right to a speedy trial is that by forcing the prosecution to try the case within a specified timeframe (this varies from state to state and can range from 90 to 180 days), the prosecution may not have sufficient time to have evidence tested and prepare their case.

Class activities

Discussion—What are society's expectations for this? What misconceptions exist in society about speedy trial and an assigned attorney?

JAIL ICON
VECTOR ILLUSTRATION

© Studio_G/Shutterstock.com

The Eighth Amendment

"Excessive bail shall not be required, nor excessive fines imposed, nor cruel and unusual punishments inflicted."

The purpose of bail is to ensure an individual will appear to answer for the charges. There is no guarantee that individuals are provided the opportunity to post bail. This denial occurs in some cases where the accused poses a threat to society or are likely to flee and have the ability to do so. Bail must be a reasonable amount that the average citizen can pay and is usually set by state statute. This is also intended to keep the defendant free and not serve time until they are convicted.

The protection against cruel and unusual punishment is intended to protect the guilty from a ghastly punishment, such as quartering, pouring boiling substances on the defendant, or other tortuous methods. The punishment must equal the crime. This also applies to some of the conditions in the correctional environment.

Class activities

Discussion—What are society's expectations for this? What misconceptions exist in society about bail amounts? What constitutes cruel punishment in modern times?

The Fourteenth Amendment

The 14th amendment is significant to the criminal justice system because it clearly outlines the protections for individuals who are born and naturalized in the United States including equal protection of the laws. This amendment ensures that no one will be deprived of their property, liberty (freedom to move about) or life without due process.

Review Questions

1. The foundation for society in the United States is the concept of a _____.

2. The _____, _____, and _____ of free speech may be regulated by the government.

3. The grand jury protection has _____ _____ applied to all of the states.

Critical Thinking Questions

Miranda Rights-What are they? What situations do they apply to? How does the media influence the perception of these rights?

Chapter 3

Gender, Sexual Preference, and Identity: The Historical Treatment

Women comprise more than 50% of the population in the United States according to the 2010 Census report. While this is just slightly more (1.6%) than the male population, women continue to face discrimination in earnings, employment, promotions and other areas. Some of the discrepancies in wages and employment are attributed to some women choosing to exit the workforce, temporarily, to care for and raise children. Often when reentering the workforce after an extended absence these women are starting at lower-level positions in comparison with those they held when they left. Regaining the positions and earnings takes time and contributes to the inequality in pay.

Try this *(for students)*

Go to http://www.census.gov/# access the quick facts located in the center of the home page and choose your state to view demographic information. You can even look at individual cities in your state.

Less than 200 years ago, women were viewed as uncivilized and irrational which allowed for women to be treated as inferior human beings. Privileges and rights that we often take for granted currently were prohibited for women until more recently. The exclusion of women continued with the adoption of the Fourteenth Amendment in 1868. This protection defined citizens and voters as male. Women were not provided legal protection, were unable to serve on juries, sue, enter into contracts, or vote. In addition, once a woman married her property became the ownership of her husband, she was dependent upon her husband, or if single, her father. A woman did not have the ability to control the wages she received, no child custody rights, and was not allowed to own property.

The United States Congress granted women the opportunity to inherit property, enter into contracts, sue and be sued with the passage of the Married Woman's Property Bill in 1857. The right to vote was not applied to women nationwide until August 26, 1920, although several states granted this privilege prior to 1920. Ironically, black men were granted the right to vote in 1870 although as noted in Chapter 4 this right was often denied for a variety of additional requirements and not fully implemented until 1965. The Wyoming territory

© Everett Historical/Shutterstock.com

was the first to grant voting rights to women over the age of 21 in 1869 which continued when Wyoming was officially admitted to the Union. Other states such as Colorado, Utah, Nevada, California, Idaho, and 15 other states continued the momentum of granting the right to vote prior to 1920.

Traditional stereotypes of women, both positive and negative, have impacted the treatment of women in society, the home, and the criminal justice system. The common stereotypes of women as passive, emotional, irrational, and nurturing continue to aid in the perpetuation of discriminatory treatment. The Equal Protection Clause of the Fourteenth Amendment was not utilized until the *Reed v. Reed* decision, 404 U.S. 71 (1971), which identified an Idaho law giving preference to males as discriminatory. Within five years discrimination based on gender was addressed again in *Craig v. Boren*, 429 U.S. 190 (1976), which required any discriminatory law to be significant to a government objective and required comprehensive justification. *Craig v. Boren* is based on the law in Oklahoma that attempted to justify prohibiting some alcohol sales to males under the age of 21 and females under the age of 18 based on traffic safety statistics.

Women as offenders and victims

The first prison for women, Mount Pleasant, opened in New York in 1835. Prior to that time and up until the early 20th century the few women who were incarcerated were housed in men's prisons. Facilities that housed women continued to be built throughout the century and currently number approximately 170 separate facilities including 28 federal prisons.

The National Crime Victimization Survey (Criminal Victimization, 2013) identified an increase in arrests for females between 2001 and 2010. Although the overall arrest rate increased by 10.5%, there was only a slight increase (0.7%) in arrests for violent crimes while juvenile arrests decreased 15.5%. There was a significant increase in arrests for property crimes (27.1%).

OFFENSE TYPE OF STATE PRISONERS BY GENDER, 2011

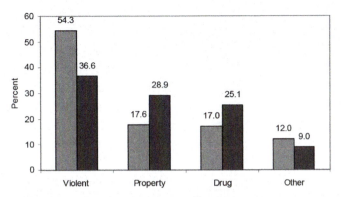

Source: Carson, A. & Sabol, W. (2012). *Prisoners in 2011.*
Washington, DC: Bureau of Justice Statistics.

NUMBER OF INCARCERATED WOMEN, 1980–2010

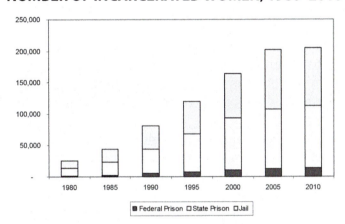

Source: Beck, A., & Karberg, J. C. (2001). *Prison and jail inmates at midyear 2000.* Washington, DC:

Bureau of Justice Statistics; Guerino, P., Harrison, P. M., & Sabol, W. (2011).
Prisoners in 2010. Washington, DC: Bureau of Justice Statistics.

Women are more likely to be victimized in their personal lives, homes, or relationships according to the 2013 Bureau of Justice Statistics report on Nonfatal Domestic Violence. In approximately 76% of domestic violence cases, the victim was a woman and the perpetrator a current or previous intimate partner. Nevada had the highest rate of women killed by men from 2003 to 2012; however, in 2012, Alaska moved ahead of Nevada for the murders of women by men.

The 2013 Bureau of Justice Statistics report on homicide revealed females were more likely to be killed within their first year of life than any other time. When looking specifically at the homicides of African-American females they were more likely to be murdered at the age of 22 followed closely by the first year of life.

In the last two decades, sexual assaults have been decreasing significantly; however, each year approximately 300,000 individuals over the age of 12 are victimized. Almost 3/4 of these crimes are committed by someone the victim knows (RAINN, 2015). For women who are Native American or of mixed race, the likelihood of being a sexual assault victim increases significantly.

Women in criminal justice

Women have fulfilled the role of "matrons" overseeing female prisoners and juveniles since the 1860s. The role of matron evolved into full-fledged corrections officers by the last half of the 20th century. In the late 1960s, females comprised approximately 12% of corrections officers. During this era, women were limited in their duties in order to reduce contact with male prisoners. In recent years, with an increase in numbers women account for almost 40% of adult corrections officers and more than half of juvenile corrections officers. Although there remain some restrictions, women are no longer limited to positions that minimize contact with male inmates.

Alice Stebbins Wells became one of the first American policewomen when she joined the Los Angeles Police Department. During this era, it was not expected for a woman to perform the same function as policemen. Wells was not armed, worked in plainclothes but had full arrest powers. Despite being limited as to the types of incidents she investigated, she made 13 arrests during her first year. Wells spoke throughout the nation in support of women joining the force which led to women being hired in 25 police departments by 1915.

Throughout the next decade women continued to join police departments; however, they were segregated into separate units and assigned "social work" duties. Discrimination was prevalent in hiring requirements that required a high school diploma for male officers and a college degree for females. Women were paid less and were required to wear skirts and heels.

This discriminatory behavior continued until the 1960s when New York City policewomen successfully sued for the opportunity to test for promotion. Affirmative action in the 1970s contributed to an increase in policewomen; however, the numbers began to decline by the 1990s. Currently approximately 12% of the police force nationwide are women. Penny Harrington was promoted to chief of the Portland Police Department (Oregon) in 1985. She became the first female to lead a major police department. Despite working her way up through the ranks since 1964 Harrington endured discriminatory behavior during her tenure as chief, leading to a lawsuit alleging bias and resignation.

Various studies have revealed female police officers are effective communicators and least likely to be accused in excessive force complaints in comparison to male counterparts. In addition, excessive force complaints and settlements are sustained against male officers at much higher rates than female officers. Women have continued to surmount obstacles in criminal justice careers; however, there continues to be issues involving discrimination, sexual and gender harassment, marginalization, and difficulties in advancing into leadership positions.

One of the first known female lawyers in the United States was Myra Bradwell. Ironically, she was denied entry to the bar despite passing the Illinois bar exam in 1869. The Supreme Court of Illinois denied her entry based upon her marital status. As a married woman her responsibilities were to her family and a career in law would interfere with this. A subsequent appeal denied her solely on the basis of being a woman. Bradwell brought the issue before the US. Supreme Court, which denied her based on gender in 1873. The state of Illinois passed legislation to prohibit career discrimination based on gender leading to the entry of Alta M. Hulett into the bar in 1873. Bradwell chose not to reapply and continued practicing law without a license until 1890 when the Illinois Supreme Court granted her a license.

© Iculig/Shutterstock.com

Sexual preference and identity

Great strides have been made in addressing equality based on sexual preference in the last four decades yet there remain significant issues to be resolved concerning these inequities. For centuries, same sex relationships have thrived in various cultures yet these individuals have been labeled as mentally ill, perverts, and sinners. Religious differences impact the perception of homosexuality, as well as the ongoing debate of whether homosexuality is a choice or genetic. The preferred terminology has evolved over time. Gay or homosexual may apply to males and females as a general term; however, homosexual women are often referred to as lesbian. Bisexual individuals can be either male or female but are attracted to both genders. A transgender is an individual who identifies as the opposite of their birth sex, yet a transsexual is someone who is undergoing or has completed a physical sex change.

The book *Sexual Behavior in the Human Male* was published in 1948 and addressed the commonality of same-sex behaviors. The author, Dr. Alfred Kinsey, asserted that about one-third of men had participated at least once in homosexual activities and about 10% of the population was homosexual. These numbers were controversial at the time and difficult to truly estimate. It is difficult to determine accurate statistics in current times when it is more acceptable to reveal this information. The Williams Institute on Sexual Orientation Law and Public Policy revealed in 2011 that more than 8% of the U.S. population has engaged in homosexual activity, yet less than 2% identify as bisexual and only 1.7% identify as either a lesbian or homosexual. In 2010, the U.S. Census counted same-sex households (610,472), whether married or not, for the first time.

Several key events propelled the gay rights movement in the 1960s and 1970s. A landmark event, Stonewall Riots, occurred in June of 1969. The Stonewall Inn, a gay bar in Greenwich Village, New York was owned and operated by the Genovese family yet did not have a liquor license, running water, or other amenities. Allegedly officers allowed the bar to continue operations in exchange for a weekly payoff. On this particular night, when officers of the NYPD entered to raid the establishment the patrons fought back and rioted for three nights. This incident sparked nationwide activism for acceptance and equal rights.

Class activities

Watch this short (9:15) documentary on the Stonewall Riots.
http://www.youtube.com/watch?v=mTujTI8rGBg

Continuing through the 1970s lesbians and homosexuals fought for equal rights. By 1970, the American Psychological Association asserted homosexuality is not a mental illness, as previously believed. Although some ground has been gained there continues to be legal discrimination, victimization, often violent, and negative stereotypes. The increased visibility and activism has led to more documented incidents of bias; however, it is unknown if this is a result of increased reporting or actual incidents.

The Hate Crime Statistics Act, passed by Congress in 1990 required data collection of crimes with evidence of prejudice based on one of the protected classes. This includes religion, ethnicity, disability, race, sexual orientation, and gender. Almost 21% of the hate crimes committed in 2013 were based on sexual orientation or identification. The majority of victims, over 60%, were homosexual males and a significant portion of these crimes were violent ranging from intimidation and assault to rape and murder. Typically the offenders were white males. There is still reluctance to report hate crimes due to mistrust of law enforcement officials based on a perceived intolerance for homosexuality, as well as the potential for consequences related to employment and custody if the victim's sexual preference is revealed. Currently arrest statistics are not broken down based on sexual orientation making it difficult to determine incarceration rates.

Same-sex marriage remains one of the most controversial issues in recent years. The first state to recognize civil unions between same-sex couples was Vermont in 2000, followed by other states. Currently same-sex marriages are recognized by the federal government for benefits and in more than 38 states and jurisdictions.

The hyper masculine environment of law enforcement and corrections has encouraged homophobia in the past. Research revealed in the 1990s and early 2000s that many officers resisted working with gay or lesbian coworkers. Although they have been present in corrections and law enforcement for many years it was not publicly acknowledged. Lesbian police officers are often more easily accepted because they are not a threat to other officers' self-image. The Los Angeles Police Department denied entry to openly gay officers until a1993 lawsuit. Since that time they have become as receptive as other major cities. Active recruitment of gay and lesbian officers began with San Francisco and New York City. More recent research has indicated that employment of gay and lesbian officers does not negatively impact the organizations. Despite this, some officers do not reveal their homosexuality for fear of negative consequences in the work environment.

Review Questions

1. What types of crimes are women most likely to be arrested and incarcerated for?

2. When is a female most likely to be killed?

3. What types of crimes are women more likely to be victims of and who commits these crimes?

4. What group has been stigmatized for centuries as sinners, perverts, and mentally ill?

5. Who is most likely to kill adult females?

Critical Thinking Questions

1. The arrest and incarceration rates for women have increased. Is this indicative an increase in crime committed by women or an increase in prosecution and incarceration?

2. Why do female officers have fewer excessive force complaints and settlements than male officers?

3. Why are white males more likely to commit hate crimes based on sexual preference and identity?

Chapter 4

The Chronicles of Immigrants

An immigrant is a person who relocates to a foreign country with the intent to live there permanently. The United States is a country mostly of immigrants; however, the acceptance of immigrants has come slowly regardless of the era. The legacy of immigration is the foundation for the United States. With the exception of the Native Americans who inhabited the land before the arrival of the early settlers and the African slaves who were forced to come here and labor for the benefit of many, most Americans share the legacy of immigration complete with the discrimination and struggles. Rarely can an individual only trace their history within these borders.

Immigration to the United States has been propelled by a combination of issues. The conditions in native countries such as persecution, war, and poverty drive many to leave their homes. They are inspired to come to the United States for opportunity, freedom, and safety. The core Protestant values of accountability, hard work, and profit remain the ideals of many who reside or immigrate to the United States. Often fear accompanies immigrants as they are believed to consume the welfare benefits and jobs of Americans.

Class activities

Have each individual trace their ancestry as far back as they can and share with the class. After everyone shares create a list to show how many are connected through their ancestors.

Native Americans

The original inhabitants of the United States are the Native Americans which include Indians and natives of Hawaii and Alaska. Native Americans have a special legal status and have played a role in the law, justice, and politics in the United States.

The colonization of America began in the late 1400s and significantly impacted the Native Americans. As European settlers arrived, differences between the cultures were evident and resulted in the loss of life for

© Leonard Zhukovsky/Shutterstock.com

many Native Americans. Some of this occurred through warfare and some through the intentional and unintentional spread of disease.

The cultural beliefs of the dominant European society and Native Americans differed leading to conflict and injustice. When European settlers began the colonization process, the Native Americans were significant resources. Their knowledge of the land and resources greatly benefited early settlers. These colonists needed the Native Americans to help provide them with shelter, food, and at times military aid. Part of the colonization process was the development of an ideology that was at first religious based then developed into a racist ideology that deemed Native Americans as "biologically inferior." Native Americans were first considered pagans, then viewed as savages, and finally violent.

The need for land by the settlers resulted in the marginalization of the Native American nations. Social disorganization and lack of control over their own lives and resources resulted in poverty for many as they were victimized by the colonists. The Native Americans already had their own process of justice and laws, yet this was not recognized by the colonists as it would jeopardize their claims to the land. Although the Native American nations signed treaties and other legal documents with the colonists these agreements were discarded when the colonists deemed it did not serve their financial or political interests. The colonists utilized laws to marginalize Native Americans and represent them as irrational and incapable. Most of the Native American nations in the East were forced to vacate their lands and relocate west of the Mississippi River as a result of the Indian Removal Act of 1830. The federal government was able to gain control of Native American lands by taking on a guardianship role as a result of the 1831 *Cherokee Nation* case. In other states, Native Americans were required to denounce their Indian identity, sever ties with their fellow Indians and become "civilized" before being allowed to vote.

European immigrants

Many of the European immigrants who relocated to the United States were victimized in their native countries and when they arrived in the United States. The Irish and Italian Catholics and Jewish were victims of discrimination for several reasons. As with their predecessors, they were willing to work for lower wages due to their poverty and their religion set them apart and led to resentment of their cultures. Some of these segments, in particular the Irish and Italians, formed groups to protect themselves resulting in some of the first organized crime groups. In the era before Prohibition, the organized crime groups were controlled by the Jewish and Irish.

Ironically near the turn-of-the-century, these groups had progressed educationally, financially and were more accepted in society as many African Americans moved to northern states. This led to conflict as the African Americans were willing to work for lower wages and fill in when union workers were striking. The same circumstances and behaviors that these groups endured due to their circumstances they now perpetuated against the African Americans.

© Everett Historical/Shutterstock.com

African Americans

"Slave codes" were utilized from the early 1600s to late 1800s to exclude slaves from the basic tenants of American life. This perpetuated their inferiority by denying rights of employment, education, voting, speech, property ownership, and representation in politics. The "slave codes" provided those who owned them to determine their fate. They were allowed to deny basic human needs, cruelly punish them and even maim or murder them with no legal sanctions.

Class activities

Watch this short clip (4:11) covering "Jim Crow" laws.
http://www.youtube.com/watch?v=ChWXyeUTKg8

"Jim Crow" laws continued the discrimination of African Americans through segregation. The restrictions included where they lived, who they associated with, schools, businesses, restrooms, where they could sit on the bus, and drinking fountains, among others. They continued to be denied the opportunity for peaceful assembly, voting, and serving on juries. Although these laws provided that African Americans have separate facilities, they often did not exist or they were substandard. If these laws were violated, punishments ranged from being beaten, castration, burning, dismemberment, shooting, or hanging. In the 20th century, many of these laws were found to be unconstitutional; however, it wasn't until the Civil Rights Act of 1964 that many of these truly ended.

Got questions? *(for students)*

Look at these cases- Brown v. Board of Education (1954), Civil Rights Act of 1964 and Loving v. Virginia (1967). Consider whether any of these laws and circumstances apply to other groups within the U.S.

Class activities

Review the case of Rosa Parks (1955). Discuss whether similar laws exist today. Explain how as a nation of laws disobeying some laws leads to change.

© Rob Wilson/Shutterstock.com

Hispanics

Santa Fe (New Mexico) became the first Spanish colony established in the United States in 1598. Mexican settlements were established in areas along our current border and Spanish settlements dotted the southeastern coastal region. Despite the long history in America,

Hispanics often were defeated when dealing with Caucasians. Significantly as a result of losing the Mexican-American war, Mexico lost almost half of its territory through the Treaty of Guadalupe Hidalgo in 1848. Approximately 80,000 individuals became citizens of the United States overnight when this was signed. Unfortunately, they were deemed second-class citizens, often deprived of their lives, property, land, and money. When Spain lost the Spanish-American war, Puerto Rico became part of the United States and the residents were now citizens. The largest single minority group in the United States has been Hispanics since 2007.

Discrimination against Hispanics exists both within their culture and outside of it. Even the name Hispanic creates controversy as it represents those of the Spanish heritage, while Latino represents those whose heritage stems from Latin American countries. The name can be used interchangeably; however, for purposes of this text the term Hispanic is used to remain consistent with the U.S. Census.

Puerto Ricans became citizens in 1917. With this privilege, they were allowed travel throughout the United States. Americans were also granted access to Puerto Rico, many have profited from business interests there, and yet high unemployment and poverty rates continue to plague Puerto Ricans even to this day.

Middle and upper-class Cubans immigrated to the United States in the 1950s to escape communism and their leader Fidel Castro. Their social class in their native country equipped them for survival and success in the United States. Although they were seldom stereotyped negatively as many of their fellow Hispanics, this created a divide between various Hispanic cultures leading to discrimination.

Class activities

Watch this video (26:53) on border stories.
http://www.youtube.com/watch?v=1PaWiYOH8O0

Asians

Asian immigration began in the 1840s when the Chinese arrived in Hawaii and on the West Coast of the continental United States. The early years of immigration provided unskilled labor for agriculture, mining, and railroad construction. Waves of Asian immigration continued often resulting in anti-Asian sentiment. The perception that Asians were bringing prostitution and opium to the country while negatively impacting wages in the United States contributed to the anti-Asian feelings. The Chinese Exclusion Act of 1882 excluded the Chinese from gaining citizenship making them the first group of immigrants to face discrimination by the U.S. Congress. This legislation halted immigration for a period of 10 years and denied citizenship to the Chinese immigrants. Similar laws took effect for Japanese immigrants. These laws would be repealed in 1943, however, not before segregating the Chinese to separate living areas and relocating Japanese-Americans to internment camps during World War II. Ironically, the Chinese living areas are now considered cultural "Chinatowns" which many other ethnicities patronize.

Class activities

Watch this short video clip (7:34) on Asian Americans.
http://www.youtube.com/watch?v=6hVlSuuaQhs

Review Questions

1. _____ & _____ cannot trace their ancestry to immigrants.

2. The first specific ethnic immigrant group to be specifically targeted for exclusion and denial of citizenship by the US Congress was the _____.

3. The largest minority group in the United States is_____.

4. This legislation is the most important law and ending discrimination _____ _____.

Critical Thinking Questions

1. Most immigrant groups were discriminated against and faced the same impoverished conditions yet with each new group entering the United States the same cycle has continued. Why?

2. Identify the various laws and elements that discriminated against the Native Americans, African Americans, Hispanics, and Asians.

Chapter 5

Race/Ethnicity and the Criminal Justice System

Race and ethnicity are often used interchangeably; however, the differences between the two are significant. When examining the relationship between race, ethnicity, and the criminal justice system, the divide is often greater. Race is generally considered to be a biological factor identifiable by physical characteristics such as skin color, bone structure, or eye color. The scientific basis of genetic differences in race is weak, except for the color of skin. Ethnicity is viewed as a sociological factor which includes how individuals identify with a community. This can include ancestry, nationality, or regional culture. Consider how South Africans might identify themselves. South African would be the ethnicity, yet Black or White might be the race. Individuals who identify as Hispanic or Latino are referring to their culture; however, in some instances, they would still be identified as White when counting crime. This creates further confusion when trying to identify victims and offenders.

The Office of Management and Budget (OMB), a subsection of the Executive Office of the President, provides oversight of the creation and application of the federal budget, including regulatory policies. As covered in previous chapters, race and ethnicity are important when considering how government funding will be utilized, whether significant opportunities have been afforded to traditionally marginalized races, or whether inequities based on race are evident. In 1997, the OMB developed categories to group U.S. citizens and noncitizens. The OMB requires individuals to identify their ethnicity as either Hispanic or non-Hispanic. Generally, Hispanic and Latino are used interchangeably to signify similar cultures. Hispanic is often used to identify individuals of Spanish descent, while Latino is the term preferred by those are descendents of Latin American heritage. For purposes of this textbook, the term Hispanic is being used in accordance with census documents; however, this does include the Spanish, Cuban, Mexican, Puerto Rican, and Central and South American cultures. Once an individual identifies their ethnicity, then they chose the race they relate to. This includes categories such as Asian, American Indian, African American, Native Hawaiian, Unknown, or White.

Class activities

Break out into small groups and complete a list of each individual's heritage including race, ethnic groups, religion, or other identifying factors. Compare this with the other groups to determine how diverse the classroom is.

Starting in 2014, the Federal Bureau of Investigation (FBI) began collecting data identifying the number of Hispanics involved in crime through the annual Uniform Crime Report (UCR). In addition, the U.S. Census Bureau is contemplating changing Hispanic to a race category versus ethnicity on the census. These initiatives (proposed or in effect) help to shed light on the experiences of Hispanics which may be quite different than those who identify as White. These discrepancies in data collection create issues when analyzing crime statistics for trends based on race or ethnicity; however, most criminal justice professionals are familiar with the various issues with victims reporting crime and the submission of the data to the FBI.

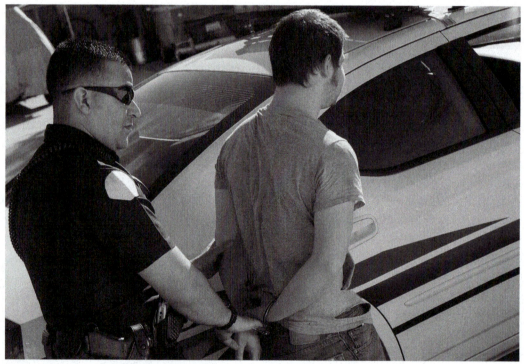

© bikeriderlondon/Shutterstock.com

Arrests

When considering the issues with data collection and crime reporting, the 2013 UCR reveals just over 9 million arrests for crimes in the United States. Over 6 million of these arrests were of White individuals and less than 800,000 were identified as Hispanic. African Americans were arrested in over 2.5 million crimes while American Indians and Asians were arrested for approximately 140,000 and 105,000 crimes, respectively. Native Hawaiians accounted for the least amount of arrests with just over 5,000. Comparing this to the

U.S. Census report, updated as of July 2013, there are currently over 320 million individuals residing in the United States. Over 200 million residents identify as White while over 40 million are of African-American heritage. Almost 46 million individuals identify as Hispanic while Asians represent almost 17 million individuals. Native Americans and native Hawaiians represent over 4 million and 1 million residents, respectively.

Got questions? *(for students)*
Are you wondering about your local community demographics? Visit the U.S. Census site covering population statistics at http://factfinder.census.gov/faces/tableservices/jsf/pages/productview.xhtml?src=bkmk

Native Hawaiians and Pacific Islanders represent the least amount of individuals arrested for any crime according to UCR data. For the remainder of this chapter, native Hawaiian arrest rates will not be included. Considering the data for sex offenses out of a total of 46,553 arrests in 2013, Whites were most likely to be arrested for this offense (33,695) followed by African Americans with11,462 arrests and over 6,000 Hispanics. American Indians were the least likely group to be arrested for sex offenses (622) followed by Asians with 744 arrests.

Rape is categorized separately than a sex offense in the UCR. In over 13,000 rapes where arrests were made, Whites were arrested more often than any other race (8,946). African Americans accounted for over 4,000) and Hispanics over 2,000. American Indians were least likely to be arrested for rape (160) followed by Asians with 173 arrests.

Murder and nonnegligent manslaughter arrests totaled 8,383 in 2013. African Americans were most likely to be arrested for these crimes (4, 379) followed closely by Whites (3,799). Hispanics were arrested in over 1,000 murderers while American Indians accounted for 98 arrests followed by Asians with 101.

Considering these statistics on aggravated assaults, once again Whites were arrested more often than any other race. Over 290,000 aggravated assaults arrests were made in 2013 and over 180,000 Whites were arrested for this offense. Just under 99,000 African Americans and over 43,000 Hispanics were arrested for aggravated assaults. American Indians were least likely (4,356) to be arrested for this offense followed closely by Asians with 4,423 arrests.

Over 78,000 arrests were made for the crime of robbery in 2013. African Americans lead the number of arrests with over 44,000 followed by almost 33,000 Whites. Hispanics accounted for over 8,000 arrests while there were 579 arrests of American Indians and 649 of Asians.

Larceny arrests accounted for 990,936 of the total crimes committed in 2013. Significantly Whites account for the majority of arrests with over 677,000, followed by African Americans with over 284,000 arrests and Hispanics with just under 63,000. Asians were least likely to be arrested with just over 12,000 followed by American Indians with over 16,000. Burglary arrests totaled over 200,000, with Whites accounting for the majority of arrests at 136,990, followed by African Americans (61,709) and Hispanics (24,035). Once again American Indians were the least likely to be arrested with just under 2,000 followed by Asians with just over 2,000 burglary arrests.

Victims

Crime victims' statistics are covered in the National Incident-Based Reporting System, a more detailed component of the UCR. In the 2013 report, the Hispanic ethnicity is not reported separately and instead combined with the White statistics. There were a total of 4,224,061 crime victims who reported these incidents to law enforcement in 2013.

Sex offenses, both forcible and nonforcible accounted for over 76,000 of these crimes. Whites were more likely to be victimized (over 58,000) followed by African Americans (over 13,000). Asians were least likely to be victims of sex offenses (approximately 550) while American Indians were victimized slightly more with almost 700 reported incidents.

In 2013, there were 3,841 reported homicide victims. African Americans accounted for 1,896 of these victims followed by Whites with 1,810. American Indians were least likely to be murdered with only 24 followed by 41 Asians.

Just under 2 million assaults were reported in 2013. Whites were most likely to be an assault victim with just under 800,000 reported followed by just over 350,000 African American victims. Asians were the least likely to be victims of assault offenses (9,336) followed by American Indians with10,087 victims. There were over 80,000 robbery victims in 2013, with once again Whites being victimized more often (46,155) followed by African Americans with just under 30,000 victims. American Indians were least likely to be the victim of a robbery (384) followed by Asians with 2,145 victims.

In 2013, there were 1,249,143 victims of larceny. Most likely to be larceny victims were Whites with just over 971,000 and African Americans with just over 181,000 victims. American Indians were least likely to be victims of larceny with just under 5,000 reported followed by Asians with just over 18,000 reported incidents. There were over half a million reported burglaries in 2013. In over 383,000 cases Whites were victimized, while African Americans accounted for just over 98,000 victims. Following the consistent crime patterns we've identified in this chapter, American Indians were least likely to be burglary victims (1,786) followed by Asians with 7,113 victims.

2013 Hate Crime Statistics

Look at Table 1 Incidents, Offenses, Victims, and Known Offenders (Hate Crimes)

TABLE 1   Incidents, Offenses, Victims, and Known Offenders by Bias Motivation, 2013

Bias motivation	Incidents	Offenses	Victims[1]	Knownoffenders[2]
Total	5,928	6,933	7,242	5,814
Single-Bias Incidents	5,922	6,921	7,230	5,808
Race:	2,871	3,407	3,563	2,733
Anti-White	653	728	754	680
Anti-Black or African American	1,856	2,263	2,371	1,747
Anti-American Indian or Alaska Native	129	146	159	108
Anti-Asian	135	158	164	130

Continued

TABLE 1   (*Continued*)

Bias motivation	Incidents	Offenses	Victims[1]	Knownoffenders[2]
Anti-Native Hawaiian or Other Pacific Islander	3	3	3	7
Anti-Multiple Races, Group	95	109	112	61
Religion:	**1,031**	**1,163**	**1,223**	**682**
Anti-Jewish	625	689	737	393
Anti-Catholic	70	74	75	72
Anti-Protestant	35	42	47	17
Anti-Islamic (Muslim)	135	165	167	127
Anti-Other Religion	117	135	137	44
Anti-Multiple Religions, Group	42	51	53	25
Anti-Atheism/Agnosticism/etc.	7	7	7	4
Sexual Orientation:	**1,233**	**1,402**	**1,461**	**1,514**
Anti-Gay (Male)	750	849	890	975
Anti-Lesbian	160	185	191	174
Anti-Lesbian, Gay, Bisexual, or Transgender (Mixed Group)	277	317	329	324
Anti-Heterosexual	21	24	24	20
Anti-Bisexual	25	27	27	21
Ethnicity:	**655**	**794**	**821**	**743**
Anti-Hispanic or Latino	331	418	432	418
Anti-Not Hispanic or Latino[3]	324	376	389	325
Disability:	**83**	**92**	**99**	**77**
Anti-Physical	22	23	24	23
Anti-Mental	61	69	75	54
Gender:	**18**	**30**	**30**	**20**
Anti-Male	5	5	5	7
Anti-Female	13	25	25	13
Gender Identity:	**31**	**33**	**33**	**39**
Anti-Transgender	23	25	25	30
Anti-Gender Non-Conforming	8	8	8	9
Multiple-Bias Incidents[4]	**6**	**12**	**12**	**6**

[1] The term *victim* may refer to a person, business, institution, or society as a whole.

[2] The term *known offender* does not imply that the identity of the suspect is known, but only that an attribute of the suspect has been identified, which distinguishes him/her from an unknown offender.

[3] The term *anti-not Hispanic or Latino* does not imply the victim was targeted because he/she was not of Hispanic origin, but it refers to other or unspecified ethnic biases that are not Hispanic or Latino.

[4] A *multiple-bias incident* is an incident in which one or more offense types are motivated by two or more biases.

Consider who (race, religion, gender, and sexual orientation) is most likely to be a victim of a hate crime? Least likely?

Look at Table 2

TABLE 2   Offenses Offense Type by Bias Motivation, 2013

Bias motivation	Total offenses	Crimes against persons							Crimes against property							Crimes against society[3]
		Murder and nonnegligent manslaughter	Rape (revised definition)[1]	Rape (legacy definition)[2]	Aggravated assault	Simple assault	Intimidation	Other[3]	Robbery	Burglary	Larceny-theft	Motor vehicle theft	Arson	Destruction/damage/vandalism	Other[3]	
Total	6,933	5	15	6	734	1,720	1,925	25	126	174	225	20	36	1,783	60	79
Single-Bias Incidents	6,921	5	15	6	733	1,717	1,922	25	125	174	225	20	36	1,779	60	79
Race:	3,407	2	7	0	398	750	1,087	15	54	91	126	11	17	759	36	54
Anti-White	728	1	6	0	79	194	155	9	24	32	75	6	4	98	17	28
Anti-Black or African American	2,263	1	0	0	288	478	829	2	23	36	16	1	11	557	7	14
Anti-American Indian or Alaska Native	146	0	0	0	11	16	26	1	3	16	27	4	0	22	10	10
Anti-Asian	158	0	1	0	15	43	43	2	4	6	5	0	2	34	2	1
Anti-Native Hawaiian or Other Pacific Islander	3	0	0	0	1	1	1	0	0	0	0	0	0	0	0	0
Anti-Multiple Races, Group	109	0	0	0	4	18	33	1	0	1	3	0	0	48	0	1
Religion:	1,163	0	1	1	23	134	255	1	3	29	38	1	17	649	6	5
Anti-Jewish	689	0	0	0	5	72	152	0	1	6	11	0	4	437	1	0
Anti-Catholic	74	0	0	0	0	6	11	0	0	6	9	0	3	36	1	2
Anti-Protestant	42	0	0	0	0	0	3	0	0	6	5	0	3	24	1	0
Anti-Islamic (Muslim)	165	0	0	1	17	41	53	0	2	2	2	0	1	43	2	1
Anti-Other Religion	135	0	1	0	1	11	26	1	0	5	4	1	5	78	1	1
Anti-Multiple Religions, Group	51	0	0	0	0	3	10	0	0	3	6	0	1	27	0	1
Anti-Atheism/Agnosticism/etc.	7	0	0	0	0	1	0	0	0	1	1	0	0	4	0	0
Sexual Orientation:	1,402	2	3	4	193	547	318	1	47	30	17	3	2	223	8	4
Anti-Gay (Male)	849	2	0	0	120	359	188	0	30	23	4	0	2	115	6	0
Anti-Lesbian	185	0	0	4	24	66	56	0	3	0	3	0	0	28	1	0

Anti-Lesbian, Gay, Bisexual, or Transgender (Mixed Group)	317	0	1	0	47	111	58	0	13	3	4	2	0	76	1	1
Anti-Heterosexual	24	0	1	0	0	6	6	1	0	3	2	0	0	2	0	3
Anti-Bisexual	27	0	1	0	2	5	10	0	1	1	4	1	0	2	0	0
Ethnicity:	794	1	1	0	103	241	235	6	15	18	23	3	0	132	7	9
Anti-Hispanic or Latino	418	1	1	0	79	118	128	0	11	9	7	1	0	55	4	4
Anti-Not Hispanic or Latino[4]	376	0	0	0	24	123	107	6	4	9	16	2	0	77	3	5
Disability:	92	0	1	0	6	16	21	2	3	5	17	1	0	11	3	6
Anti-Physical	23	0	1	0	1	5	5	0	2	0	6	0	0	2	1	0
Anti-Mental	69	0	0	0	5	11	16	2	1	5	11	1	0	9	2	6
Gender:	30	0	2	0	2	19	2	0	0	0	2	1	0	1	0	1
Anti-Male	5	0	0	0	1	1	0	0	0	0	1	1	0	1	0	0
Anti-Female	25	0	2	0	1	18	2	0	0	0	1	0	0	0	0	1
Gender Identity:	33	0	0	1	8	10	4	0	3	1	2	0	0	4	0	0
Anti-Transgender	25	0	0	0	8	7	4	0	3	1	0	0	0	2	0	0
Anti-Gender Non-Conforming	8	0	0	1	0	3	0	0	0	0	2	0	0	2	0	0
Multiple-Bias Incidents[5]	12	0	0	0	1	3	3	0	1	0	0	0	0	4	0	0

[1] The figures shown in this column for the offense of rape include only those reported by law enforcement agencies that used the revised Uniform Crime Reporting (UCR) definition of rape. See the data declaration for further explanation.

[2] The figures shown in this column for the offense of rape include only those reported by law enforcement agencies that used the legacy UCR definition of rape. See the data declaration for further explanation.

[3] Includes additional offenses collected in the National Incident-Based Reporting System. See Methodology.

[4] The term anti–not Hispanic or Latino does not imply the victim was targeted because he/she was not of Hispanic origin, but it refers to other or unspecified ethnic biases that are not Hispanic or Latino.

[5] A multiple-bias incident is an incident in which one or more offense types are motivated by two or more biases.

Consider who (race, religion, gender, and sexual orientation) is most likely to be a victim of rape (revised and legacy definition), homicide, simple assault, aggravated assault, and vandalism?

Class activities

The original brown eyed blue-eyed experiment was modified it conducted with college students. View the following clips:
https://www.youtube.com/watch?v=-pv8mCHbOrs (part 1)
https://www.youtube.com/watch?v=5mp5Hs4eafU (part 2)

Discuss as a class the differences in this experiment versus the original? Does the age of the participants impact the results? Clearly we are observing college students in a different decade, are there experiences similar to what we observed in the previous experiment?

CJ professionals

Statistics on criminal justice professionals are collected in respect to some professions, however, not in all. The Census of State and Local Law Enforcement agencies is conducted every four years by the U.S. Department of Justice. According to the most recent report, the proportion of sworn minority officers in local police departments has slightly increased to 25.3% in 2007 (U. S. Department of Justice, 2010). One of the first recognized African American police officers was Samuel Battle of the New York City Police Department. Despite discrimination challenges Battle in 1926, became the first African American sergeant in NYPD. Battle continued his progression through the ranks becoming the first African American lieutenant, and the first African American parole commissioner. Although he retired in 1951, the city renamed the corner of West 135th Street and Lenox Avenue as the Samuel J. Battle Plaza to recognize his contributions. Ironically in 1919 at that particular corner, there was a racial skirmish and Battle saved a life of a White officer during this incident.

Thurgood Marshall was denied admission to the University of Maryland Law School in 1930 based on his race. Fortunately, he attended Howard University Law School that same year and his first major case was a successful suit to allow an African American man admittance to a university. Ironically in this 1933 case, the defendant was the University of Maryland. Marshall continued his prominent career focused on civil rights including the 1954 *Brown v. Board* decision. Marshall was appointed to the U.S. Court of Appeals for the Second Circuit by John F. Kennedy. Although he delivered over 150 decisions related to Fourth Amendment issues, immigrant rights, and privacy issues, out of the 98 majority decisions the U.S. Supreme Court did not reverse a single case. In 1967, Thurgood Marshall became the first African American Justice appointed to the U.S. Supreme Court.

© Ritu Manoj Jethani/Shutterstock.com

Other notable minority criminal justice professionals include Fred Lau who became the first Asian American police chief in 1996 when he was selected to head the San Francisco Police Department. Upon his retirement in 2002, he became the Transportation Security Administration Federal Security Director at the San Francisco International Airport. Shortly after Lau's retirement, in 2004, Heather Fong became SFPD's first Asian American female police chief. In 2009, Sonia Sotomayor became the first Hispanic woman appointed to the United States Supreme Court.

© K2 images/Shutterstock.com

Review Questions

1. What is a hate crime?

2. What race is most likely to be a victim of a hate crime? Least likely?

3. What religion is most likely to be a victim of a hate crime? Least likely?

4. What gender is most likely to be a victim of a hate crime? Least likely?

5. What sexual orientation is most likely to be a victim of a hate crime? Least likely?

Critical Thinking Questions

1. When looking at the arrest data from 2013 what conclusions can you draw from this information?

2. Look at the National Crime Victimization Survey data and compare that with the information from the National Incident-Based Reporting System victimization reports. How different are the statistics? What accounts for these differences?

3. African American, Hispanic, Asian and American Indian criminal justice professionals have increased in numbers yet are still the minority in the criminal justice system. What difficulties are there in recruiting, hiring, and retaining these demographics?

Chapter 6

Juveniles and the CJ System

Children have a unique role in society and the criminal justice system. Leading up to the 1800s the period of what we now consider childhood was limited. At a young age children were a fundamental part of the family's economic survival. Families that depended on agriculture utilized children as labor. Industrialization led to more work inside factories where children were the preferred labor due to being inexpensive and unlikely to strike.

Opposition to child labor began emerging in the early 1800s out of a desire to avoid endangering their health. Massachusetts advanced child labor issues with the passing of the first state child labor law in 1836. This law mandated school attendance for at least three months a year for children under the age of fifteen. By 1842, Massachusetts and other states had implemented laws limiting a child's workday to 10 hours, though enforcement of this law was rare. Over the next 96 years, various laws were passed limiting employment based on age. Many of these were overturned, rewritten, passed, and overturned again. Finally, the Fair Labor Standards Act was passed in 1938 regulating child labor for the first time.

Houses of refuge

Juveniles were incarcerated in jails and penitentiaries during the late 18th and early 19th century, often with hardened adult criminals or those who were mentally ill, due to a lack of facilities for youths. Not all of these children were incarcerated due to criminal behavior; there was simply a lack of options for dealing with poverty and neglect. The Society for the Prevention of Pauperism originated with Thomas Eddy and John Griscom, and focused on establishing an institution that separated adults from juveniles who were incarcerated for criminal behavior and housed the needy children that potentially were on the path to a life of crime. Through this work, the first institution, The New York House of Refuge was opened in 1825. Boston and Philadelphia followed suit within a few years and throughout the country similar institutions opened. Throughout the years, the conditions in these institutions worsened with overcrowding and abuse. The movement for public schools and education requirements changed the direction of the Houses of Refuge when education was emphasized. The new institutions which provided training were called reform schools and in current times referred to as youth correctional institutions.

© sakhorn/Shutterstock.com

Juvenile court

Juveniles were tried in adult courts until the end of the 19th century. The belief that youths' moral and cognitive capacities had not developed fully prompted the reform of juvenile justice. A variety of methods were used to address youth problems, including probation and an out of home placement. These programs and institutions helped create the first juvenile court in 1899 in Chicago, IL.

The legal doctrine *parens patriae* (the State as Parent) became the foundation of the juvenile justice system. This provided the court with the power to provide protective supervision and rehabilitation when deemed necessary and included youths in need of services as well as delinquents.

The effectiveness of the juvenile justice system was called into question by the mid-20th century. The discretion of the juvenile court judges created inconsistency in the treatment or sanctions. Youths were often at the mercy of the judge and sanctions based on the judges' values or whims were applied unequally. The Supreme Court ruled on a variety of cases in the 1960s that led to checks and balances within the juvenile justice system by formalizing juvenile courts as well as providing due process protections to youths. The focus of the juvenile justice system remained on rehabilitation.

Two of the key cases that impacted the juvenile justice system in the 1960s were *Kent v. United States* (1966) *and In re Gault* (1967). Most states consider someone under the age of 18 to be a juvenile, although a few states have lowered this to age 16. The right to a hearing in juvenile court before a judicial waiver moving the case to an adult court was granted under *Kent v. United States* (1966). *In re Gault* (1967) provided several rights consistent with the due process for adults. Before a juvenile could be incarcerated, they were granted the right to counsel, to be notified of the charges, the opportunity to confront witnesses, Fifth Amendment protections against self-incrimination, and the right to an appeal. In the 1970s, juveniles were granted the same adult standard of "proof beyond a reasonable doubt" and protections against double jeopardy limiting a case to be tried in either juvenile or adult court, but not both.

The public perception of an increase in juvenile crime coupled with a lenient system prompted stricter laws and sentencing as well as mandatory adult charges for certain crimes in the 1980s. During this time period serious cases often warranted detention prior to a trial. The focus on punishment increased in the 1990s with stricter sanctions and an increase in confinement. Ultimately, this led to a reversal of focus back on rehabilitation by the end of the 20th century. The impact of the get tough tactics led to decisions limiting the death penalty to those over 18 as well as removing life sentences without the possibility of parole for juveniles. Some constitutional rights that differ from adults are the standard of reasonable suspicion in a school search and bench trials as opposed to a jury trial.

Class activities

Read about Sara Kruzen and view the brief video to learn more about life sentences without parole (http://www.eurthisnthat.com/2009/10/27/life-sentences-for-juveniles-yes-or-no-video/). Discuss as a class this sentence and the eventual release of Sara.

The majority of states impose a minimum age limit, usually between 6 and 8, as a guide for competence to commit criminal acts. This is based on the premise that *mens rea* cannot be formed by young children. Individuals committing crimes under the "age of reason" are often addressed utilizing therapeutic models. In Nevada children between the ages of 8 and 10 cannot be charged with a crime unless it is murder or certain sex offenses. For those between the ages of 8 and 13 evidence must demonstrate knowledge of the wrongful behavior before criminal proceedings can be pursued. With the exception of sex and firearms charges most crimes committed by someone under 18 falls under the jurisdiction of juvenile court. However, regardless of age, if a murder is committed this is adjudicated in adult courts.

Juvenile offenders

Despite an increase in juvenile crime during the last decades of the 20th century, in particular of homicides, juvenile crime has consistently decreased. According to the Uniform Crime Report in 2013, there were 875,262 arrests of individuals under the age of 18 with over 6,000 arrests under the age of 10. The majority of arrests for those under the age of 18 were for property crimes and thefts while for those under the age of 10 the majority of arrests were for assaults followed by property crimes.

Juveniles as victims

The 2013 National Incident Based Reporting System (NIBRS) reveals almost 300,000 juveniles were crime victims. They were most likely to be victims of crimes against their person with assaults (161,248) followed by sex offenses, both forcible and nonforcible (48,703). Almost 50,000 juveniles were victims of theft. The numbers for juvenile victims under the age of 10 are alarming with 40,794 victims of assault and almost 20,000 victims of forcible and nonforcible sex offenses. Theft was the leading property crime were juvenile victims with almost 5,000 victims.

Juveniles as criminal justice professionals

Although formal careers are not attainable for those under the age of 18, several initiatives provide for the involvement of juveniles in the judicial process. One of these programs is teen court. This program provides an opportunity for first-time offenders to be judged by their peers instead of being processed in juvenile court. The offender must admit guilt in order to be eligible for this. Other teens take on the role of prosecutor, defense attorney, bailiff, and jurors to determine what sanctions shall apply to the offender. This program provides the opportunity for youths who are interested in careers within the criminal justice system to perform community service in these roles.

Got questions? *(for students)*

Visit this site to learn more about "Teen Court"http://www.sa18.state.fl.us/page/teen-court-peer-court.html. A similar program, Trial by Peers is operated in Las Vegas, NV.
http://www.clarkcountylawfoundation.org/peer_counselors.html

Review Questions

1. Although children are now valued, prior to the 19th century they were viewed as _____.

2. *Parens patriae* means _____.

3. The first juvenile court opened in _____ in Illinois.

4. Juveniles usually cannot be criminally prosecuted under the ages of _____ (varies state to state).

5. Children were the preferred labor in the 18th century due to being _____ and unlikely to _____.

Critical Thinking Questions

1. The New York House of Refuge opened in 1825 to provide what services to youths?

2. What protections resulted from the *in re Gault* (1967) case?

Chapter 7

Mental Illness and the Criminal Justice System

Each year mental illness affects approximately 44 million adults in the United States. The costs of mental illness are difficult to determine because this reaches across so many aspects of society. Serious mental illness costs over $193 billion dollars just in lost earnings and it is estimated that the costs of treating mental illness is over $300 billion a year in the United States. One in five adults and children suffer from a mental illness. Mental illness is evident in over half of those affected by the age of 14 and by age 24 over 75% of mental illness conditions have developed.

The Community Mental Health Act became law in late 1963. This act is also known as the Mental Retardation and Community Mental Health Centers Construction Act of 1963. Several significant changes to the treatment of those who have been diagnosed as mentally ill resulted from this legislation. One of the most important actions changed the treatment of mentally ill individuals to a community-based program. Prior to this time, many individuals diagnosed with a mental illness were kept in hospitals or psychiatric wards. The development of various medications and therapies to treat mental illnesses provided evidence that effective treatment occurred when an individual was back in their home community. This led to a significant deinstitutionalization of the mentally ill. However, over the last five decades, the impact of this shift, along with other factors, has led to an increase of interaction between those suffering from a mental illness and the criminal justice system.

Mental illness is connected to all segments of the criminal justice system in varying degrees. This requires criminal justice practitioners to develop an understanding of the issues related to the illness in order to address the situation at hand and protect both the individual and society. This may begin with the gatekeepers of the criminal justice system, law enforcement, who frequently respond to service calls to aid those who appear to be suffering from a mental illness, whether diagnosed or not. The majority of these calls may be service related versus crime related; however, service calls can quickly escalate to a situation that involves a

© littleny/Shutterstock.com

crime or act of violence. Notably law enforcement frequently interacts with the homeless. Over a quarter of the homeless in shelters suffer from a mental illness; this does not take into account those who are living on the street. Once the situation is identified as a crime and the individual is arrested the courts begin to consider the diagnosis of mental illness or disorders, and the relationship to the criminal act. When corrections staff is tasked with the control and treatment of those with a mental illness, the response to these individuals is significant in maintaining a safe environment for prisoners and staff. Almost a quarter of those incarcerated in a state facility suffer from a mental illness.

Class activities

Ask the class to identify types of mental illnesses and estimate how much of the population is affected by them. Discuss the class perceptions.

Mental illness is a label frequently used to describe individuals who deviate from social norms, whether or not there is any actual diagnosis. When people consider some criminal acts there is frequently speculation about the mental status depending upon the details of the crimes that were committed. This provides a way to explain horrific acts such as dismembering bodies, consuming body parts, or raping or murdering children. In March of 2015 an 18-year-old North Carolina resident stabbed a family of five. Although the mother and 14-year-old daughter survived the attack the three boys, ages 1, 5, and 12, were brutally stabbed to death. "Crazy" is the term that is used to describe the eighteen year old murderer. How else could you explain murdering a 1-year-old?

Got questions? *(for students)*

Do you want to know more about this case? Go to http://abcnews.go.com/US/wireStory/police-juveniles-stabbed-death-north-carolina-home-29720813

Generally mental illness is defined as a disruption of thoughts, behaviors, and moods, according to the American Psychiatric Association. This includes disorders such as depression, anxiety, attention deficit hyperactivity disorder (ADHD), autism spectrum disorder (ASD), bipolar disorder, borderline personality disorder (BPD), dissociative disorders, eating disorders, obsessive-compulsive disorder, post-traumatic stress disorder (PTSD), Schizoaffective disorder. Some of these illnesses are unlikely to be significant in any interactions with the criminal justice system; however, they may affect treatment in the correctional system.

Depression and mood disorders are the most common mental illnesses and may require law enforcement interaction in order to determine services, such as medical treatment after a suicide attempt or a civil commitment if the individual appears to be a danger to themselves, others, or appears to be incapable of taking care of themselves. A civil commitment (a Legal 2000 in Nevada and a Baker Act in Florida) is enacted by a law enforcement officer or medical doctor and the individual is observed for up to 72 hours during which a psychiatric evaluation is conducted to establish what treatment if any should be applied or if the individual remains a threat to themselves or others. The courts would have less impact

on matters concerning depression and mood disorders. Unless there are issues related to a civil commitment, mitigating or aggravating circumstances are most likely to be considered by the courts. This may occur with the decision to prosecute or offer a plea, or sentencing considerations. For those under the umbrella of corrections, again these disorders are only significant when it comes to the treatment and safety of the individual and staff. Medical staff in correctional institutions disperse medications for these conditions and provide medical care. Correctional staff ensures the safety of individuals who appear to have suicidal thoughts, or have made attempts while in the facility. For individuals under the supervision of a probation or parole officer, it is important for those officers to understand the role the illness may play in rehabilitating the individual and their ability to reenter society.

Psychotic disorders involve the thought processes or rather the disruption of those. Schizophrenia, a psychotic disorder, includes hallucinations that are seen or heard by only the individual affected. For law-enforcement officers responding to incidents involving those who are suffering from these disorders, great care must be taken to ensure the safety of everyone involved. The individual may not respond to officer direction and instead be threatened by the officer, especially if the hallucinations or voices are indicating the officer means harm. A well-known case involving a diagnosed Paranoid Schizophrenic is the "Son of Sam" murders. In the 1970s, David Berkowitz attacked 15 individuals resulting in six murders. Berkowitz had claimed he was commanded to attack by his neighbor's dog. The schizophrenia played a small role during the investigative process, however, became a more significant concern when the case was before the courts. Although he was diagnosed as insane, during a competency hearing medical professionals deemed his diagnosis did not interfere with his fitness to stand trial. Berkowitz pled guilty to the six murders and has been incarcerated since 1978. Although he later recanted his possession claims, he has been under psychiatric care in the correctional system.

Got questions? *(for students)*

Do you want to know more about this case? Go to http://www.biography.com/people/david-berkowitz-9209372

Several different mental illnesses, bipolar, BPD, obsessive- compulsive, dissociative or ADHD, may impact criminal behavior, however, do not play a significant role in the investigation or judicial aspects of the case. Bipolar disorder impacts an individual's ability to think clearly, as well as their mood and energy. BPD includes mood swings that are severe, stormy relationships, instability, and impulsive behavior. Obsessive- compulsive disorder includes intrusive thoughts and urges to engage in repetitive actions. Dissociative disorders affect self-perception and memory of an individual. ADHD includes hyperactivity and impulsive, uncontrollable behavior. The symptoms of these illnesses may be used as mitigating factors when considering sentencing; however the majority of these illnesses are a concern for corrections. Despite various therapies, including medication, these illnesses are likely to impact the interaction between inmates and correctional staff. Certainly they may not be as obvious as someone who is suffering from hallucinations, yet the impulsiveness, instability, severe mood swings, repetitive compulsions, and volatile behaviors can significantly impact the inmate "society" and the safety of everyone within the walls of the correctional facility. For probation or parole officers these disorders, if untreated, may increase the difficulties for an individual to maintain employment and relationships, which in turn affects their rehabilitation and potentially their status in probation or parole.

Dementia covers a variety of conditions related to difficulties with memory, recognition, language and motor function. Generally this affects individuals as they age. Dementia symptoms can be caused by other disorders or illnesses such as when the oxygen supply is cut off or reduced to the brain, various cardiac conditions, strokes, brain tumors, reactions to medications, and toxins. One of the most common forms of dementia is Alzheimer's disease. This progressive condition starts with memory loss and affects the ability to think coherently and make decisions. As Alzheimer's progresses the affected have difficulty carrying out routine, daily activities and often do not recognize their loved ones. Although medical professionals recommend a variety of activities to slow the progression of this disease, there is no known cure at this time. This disease generally afflicts those over the age of 60; however, the incidence of cases greatly increases with age. Currently approximately over 5 million Americans have been diagnosed with Alzheimer's and it is the sixth leading cause of death in this country. Due to the aging population the number of Americans suffering from this illness are expected to increase to over 10 million in the next three decades.

Often law enforcement interacts with Alzheimer's sufferers when they are confused, lost, or committing traffic infractions. Due to the symptoms of Alzheimer's some incidents may involve an alleged criminal activity, such as theft when an individual forgets to pay for an item or simple battery if the individual become combative. More often law enforcement responds to individuals with Alzheimer's in a service role. These situations can quickly escalate if the individual becomes confused or frightened. In the courts, the significance of the behaviors related to Alzheimer's would be critical in determining whether intent exists in order to prosecute a crime, such as in a shoplifting case. If a crime is prosecuted, the Alzheimer's diagnosis may be used as a mitigating factor for sentencing. Certainly this is significant for corrections, especially with an increase in the incarceration of elderly individuals. This requires specialized care to address the symptoms and behaviors appropriately. When an individual is frightened because they do not know who they are or where they are they may be combative with correctional staff or other inmates.

Class activities

As a class view this video (the incident occurs approximately 19 minutes in) and discuss the role Alzheimer's could play in this situation, as well as appropriate law enforcement responses. https://www.youtube.com/watch?v=9Fk6GFiUa9c

Autism is identified under mental illnesses and disorders; however, some organizations dispute the mental illness label and instead assert that autism is a neurological disorder that affects the functioning of the brain. Regardless, autism affects the ability to socialize and communicate with others. The autism spectrum includes a variety of behaviors and degrees of these behaviors. Law enforcement may deal with autistic individuals when their behaviors invite closer inspection. Consider a teenage autistic male who frequently removes his clothing. This would be viewed and addressed differently within the confines of the family and immediate social circle, however if this occurs in public, it may involve a law-enforcement response. The lack of intent would be critical for most incidents, yet there remain difficulties dependent upon the circumstances of each case.

Imagine an autistic individual in their 20s who damages their neighbor's property. This may be worked out between neighbors or require law-enforcement intervention. The difficulty becomes in how to address or prevent future incidents. If the autistic neighbor repeatedly throws a ball through a window, how does the neighbor or parents/caregivers of the autistic individual prevent future occurrences? What occurs when the autistic adult frequently peers into the neighbor's window? Even more importantly is the response of law enforcement officers when dealing with an autistic individual. The difficulties in communication, lack of understanding an officer's words or instructions, the sensitivity to sound, lights, or pain, may increase the individual's agitation if law enforcement or medical providers are responding to treat the individual. Some cases involving autistic individuals are addressed in the criminal justice system, as the harm sometimes necessitates this. This becomes difficult to navigate in the judicial system when determining intent and ability, but is often more difficult under the corrections aspect. In one Maryland case an 18-year-old autistic man was arrested for battering a police officer and committed battery of a corrections officer while incarcerated. An autistic individual would need to be treated in a medical unit, and likely in isolation, in order to protect the individual and others.

Got questions? *(for students)*

Curious about Autism and law enforcement go to http://www.officer.com/article/10880086/law-enforcement-and-autism. For additional information on the above case go to http://www.washingtonpost.com/opinions/an-autistic-man-caught-in-the-criminal-justice-system/2014/12/07/2d2af6b8-7b42-11e4-b821-503cc7efed9e_story.html

PTSD results from a traumatic event which includes a violent act, an accident, or military combat. In recent years, society has become more aware of PTSD, especially for military veterans. According to the Mayo Clinic, PTSD symptoms may include to varying degrees intrusive memories, avoidance, or negative changes in thinking and mood, or emotional reactions. In the last three decades, victim advocacy groups and mental healthcare professionals have recognized the occurrence of PTSD in violent crime victims. Naturally, this becomes another area in which law enforcement must be educated in order to respond efficiently and safely to incidents involving someone with PTSD. A crime victim may not respond in an ordinary manner if they suffer from PTSD. Routine interaction with veterans suffering from PTSD may quickly escalate into use of force situations. The courts must be aware of the intricacies of PTSD when accommodating a crime victim who may be required to testify, or when considering any mitigating circumstances during a trial or sentencing.

Veterans become involved in the criminal justice system for a variety of reasons, some related to PTSD and others may be related to substance abuse issues. With the awareness of PTSD in veterans, the first court for veterans opened in 2008, in New York. This is similar to a drug court where treatment or mental health treatment is often an alternative. The concept creates an opportunity for criminal justice professionals who are knowledgeable in the many aspects of PTSD for veterans to provide comprehensive treatment and sanctions.

Got questions? *(for students)*

Curious about what is considered a mental illness? PTSD? Go to http://www.nami.org/ or http://www.mayoclinic.org/diseases-conditions/post-traumatic-stress-disorder/basics/definition/con-20022540.

The increase of interactions between law enforcement and those suffering from a mental illness have resulted in increased training both in the police academy and in-service training. These efforts aim to increase the effectiveness when dealing with situations involving mental illness. In the late 1980s, the increase of incidents involving the police response and mental illness necessitated the development of programs that provided service and treatment to the unique population. Often these crises resulted in the use of force or deadly force for law enforcement. Lieutenant Sam Cochran of the Memphis Police Department (Tennessee) initiated a partnership with mental health professionals and universities in the area to develop a program for first responders known as Crisis Intervention Team (CIT). CIT has earned national and international recognition and provides the foundation for similar programs in many other police agencies throughout the world. These programs contribute to a greater knowledge of mental illness, understanding of the issues, and methods to ensure the safety of the officer and citizens involved in these incidents.

Many agencies utilize either a team or specially trained officers to respond to crises involving the mentally ill. The Las Vegas Metropolitan Police Department created a Crisis Intervention Team (CIT) in 2002 to assist individuals in an unstable crisis or those with a mental illness. The CIT works with law enforcement and the community to resolve crisis situations with respect and understanding towards the afflicted and their families. Often law enforcement officers refer those affected by a mental illness to treatment facilities or other social service agencies that can provide assistance. In addition to a team, many officers within the agency undergo the training and serve as CIT officers on their various squads.

This allows for officers who are in the field to respond quickly to dynamic situations and help to de-escalate the crises and provide alternatives to incarceration when possible.

In the Las Vegas metropolitan area, there were over 40 officer involved shootings between 1991 and 2015 that resulted in the mentally ill suspect being shot. Some of these incidents were unavoidable such as a case where the parent of a mentally ill individual contacted law enforcement believing the adult sons suffering from mental illness was going to harm the parent. As is often the case less than lethal weapons such as pepper spray, a Taser, and police canines were ineffective in restraining the man who managed to attack one officer with a knife before being fatally shot. In several other incidents, officers fatally shot individuals suffering from mental illness when they held knives to the throats of the potential victims.

One controversial incident involving an unarmed veteran who suffered from PTSD occurred in December of 2011. Stanley Gibson was a disabled Gulf War veteran who had been experiencing difficulties related to PTSD. Gibson's disability benefits had been reduced in previous years and were eliminated by the Veterans Administration approximately 2 weeks before his death. As a result of the loss of benefits, Gibson also had been removed from the anti-anxiety medication.

On December 11, 2011, Gibson experienced a breakdown and reportedly did not know where he was or what he was doing. He stood in his front yard screaming at passing cars. When police arrived Gibson allegedly took a fighting stance and resisted arrest. Officers at the scene took him into custody under a Legal 2000. Instead of being held for 72 hours, Gibson was released after eight hours. The next morning, December 12, 2011, Gibson called 911 on two occasions requesting medical assistance, then drove to a hospital but left without receiving treatment. Later that evening, around 9:30 PM, Gibson called his wife to say he was outside their condo; however, he was mistakenly at the condo complex next door. Around the same time officers working in the area looking a burglary suspect. Gibson, who appeared lost and confused, was circling the parking lot. Officers surrounded Gibson's vehicle; however, Gibson accelerated and spun his wheels unsuccessfully trying to get away. He refused to get out of the vehicle and officers negotiated with him for approximately a half-hour to no avail. Officers decided to shoot a less than lethal beanbag shotgun at a window in the vehicle and then use pepper spray to force Gibson out. Due to miscommunication in the planning and execution of this strategy, an officer heard the beanbag gun being fired and believed Gibson was firing on officers. This officer fired seven times at Gibson and killed him.

Review Questions

1. Mental illness affects approximately _____ adults in the United States.

2. Mental illness is evident in over half of those affected by the age of _____.

3. What is CIT?

4. _____ is defined as a disruption of thoughts, behaviors, and moods.

5. This progressive condition starts with memory loss and affects the ability to think coherently and make decisions-_____.

6. _____ disorder includes mood swings that are severe, stormy relationships, instability, and impulsive behavior.

7. _____ affects the ability to socialize and communicate with others.

8. _____ is a psychotic disorder, includes hallucinations that are seen or heard by only the individual affected.

9. _____ results from a traumatic event which includes a violent act, an accident, or military combat.

10. The _____ court creates an opportunity for criminal justice professionals who are knowledgeable in the many aspects of PTSD to provide comprehensive treatment and sanctions.

Critical Thinking Questions

1. How did the Community Mental Health Act (1963) impact the criminal justice system in the past and currently?

2. Why are the costs of mental illness difficult to determine?

3. What is mental illness? What circumstances should a defendant not be held accountable for criminal acts based on their illness?

4. What types of mental illnesses are likely to result in interaction with the criminal justice system?

Chapter 8

Social Class: Does it Affect Justice?

Social class is another form of identifying differences in society. Generally, social class refers to the economic, educational, or social class that individuals identify with. This may include distinct characteristics, culture, gender, age, race, or interests. A hierarchy is evident with one class being perceived as more important than another, often based on economic status; however, in some instances, it may be based on other attributes.

Class activities

In small groups, identify what social classes exist within your immediate community and throughout the United States, compare with the other class groups.

When it comes to working classes, unskilled laborers are usually paid the least and at the bottom of the hierarchy and considered the lower class, have little income or property and do not significantly impact law or government. Skilled laborers often are called the working class, and may include professions that provide a substantial income such as building contractors, mechanics, or plumbers. The middle class often incorporates those with education and greater earning potential. The upper class is limited to those with substantial financial resources who exert influence in government and law. These generalities may take on different significance depending upon each culture. The criminal class is another form of difference used to divide groups between law-abiding citizens and criminals.

Social class impacts the criminal justice system in a variety tangible and intangible ways. Laws and policies are shaped by society; however, many believe the upper class, and middle-class to some extent, hold the power to influence what is considered criminal behavior and what sanctions are expected. Conflict theorists would argue this is a way of controlling the lower classes. To some, this can be evident in different classifications of crimes as "white-collar" or "street crimes" and punishments.

White-collar crimes generally are not the focus of the criminal justice system, often due to the lack of physical or psychological harm. Many white-collar crimes involve aspects that society is generally unaware of, such as dumping toxic chemicals into residential areas,

© bestv/Shutterstock.com

financial crimes where the victim played some role in allowing perpetrators to commit their crime, or the impact is not immediate and severe. For example, fraudulently obtaining financial aid appears to only impact the government. For this reason, many people do not consider it a serious crime. However, when society looks at what occurs when this is discovered the real harm may be evident with the decreased resources to help those in need, the impact on organizations that have to repay the federal government, the costs to employers to implement strategies to deter these types of criminal acts, and to monitor processes to ensure the organization is not victimized again. The ponzi schemes, where an individual invests money with an individual or group and that is used to pay other investors creating a cycle, is another example. If an individual in their 50s invested $200,000 in retirement income that was used to pay another investor, the effect is not immediately evident. Some would argue the individual had the money to lose for investment; however, the crime may impact the mental health of the victim, the ability to maintain their employment, health, or household. This may turn into a need for government assistance in their retirement years, and impacts much of society in a cycle.

© mangostock/Shutterstock.com

Street crimes, on the other hand, are frequently the topic of news headlines because of the notoriety or ability to inflict harm on others. This is often the focus during elections or proposed legislation. Some believe this is another way to incarcerate the lower classes who are believed to be more likely to commit these types of crimes. An important distinction is that many of the street crimes, such as battery, robbery, homicide, do result in immediate physical harm to the individual or the loss of life. This differs from white-collar crimes significantly; however, the harm from both street and white-collar crimes can be catastrophic.

The role of capitalism in American society helps perpetuate the cycle where some will earn or inherit more than others. A variety of factors influence this; however, research has demonstrated that children who are exposed to developmental experiences, high-quality education, and come from a financially advantaged life style will generally perform well in school, continue their education, and attain better employment leading to acquiring greater wealth. Individuals, who did not grow up in these types of households, generally do not perform as well in school, leading to lower levels of employment and acquisition of financial stability. The Department of Health and Human Services establishes the poverty level throughout the United States. This differs in some areas such as Hawaii, Alaska, and Washington, D.C.; however, for 2015 an individual head of household who earns less than $$11,770 is considered impoverished. For a family of two, poverty is an annual income under $15,930, a family of three, under $20,090 and for a family of four under $24,250.

The inequities between classes can be strengthened or relieved by government policy. With taxable income, the government is able to fund programs that help the less advantaged members of society. Preventative and punitive strategies utilized by government programs can impact criminal behavior. Preventive strategies such as income credits, housing assistance, preschool education for less advantaged children, free or reduced breakfasts and lunches and schools, reduced or free health care, and so on are all aimed at decreasing income disparity, which is often linked to criminal behavior. On the other hand, punitive strategies such as mandatory sentencing, get tough strategies, increased criminalization of narcotics and limitations on treatment and rehabilitation programs within the correctional system may increase the negative impacts of income disparity.

A variety of theories offer perspectives on the relationship between criminal behavior and social class. Individual defect theories placed the blame of criminal behavior with the individual and family. If the family does not teach moral and acceptable behaviors and accountability to the next generation, criminal behavior is the likely result. Social interaction theories place the blame on the criminal justice system for criminalizing certain behaviors, focusing on lower income communities, and labeling those from disadvantaged homes as criminals at a young age. Structural outcome theories identified the emotional and physical stresses of inequality and poverty as a cause of criminal behavior. This is perpetuated by individuals who want financial advantages but lack the resources or ability to obtain them for themselves, so they use criminal behavior to obtain.

A frequent myth perpetuated by the media is that the lower class preys on the upper class. The reality is those from a lower socioeconomic class engage in criminal behavior relatively close to home, therefore victimizing other lower-class individuals. For the criminal justice system, social class or wealth becomes controversial once an individual enters the criminal justice system. The perception exists that money can buy an excellent defense attorney, pay off corrupt officials and lead to a lack of prosecution or few sanctions. In some cases, there is support for these perceptions, such as a wealthy or high profile defendant who can pay for the best team of defense lawyers. Many individuals perceive the court appointed public

© Tashatuvango/Shutterstock.com

defender to be overwhelmed with cases and unable to devote significant time to defending the financially disadvantaged client. It should be noted that each state and jurisdiction differs in the qualifications that results in being appointed a public defender. Often public defenders have developed better working relationships with prosecutors to negotiate a plea when it is unlikely they will be successful at trial based on the evidence. In addition, due to a number of cases before a particular judge, the public defender has the opportunity to develop various strategies to aid in the defense of a client. The belief, real or imagined, that "you get what you pay for" is evident when discussing social class, wealth and the criminal justice system.

Try this

Who qualifies for a public defender? Locate resources from your local public defender's office to determine what the qualifications are to be "appointed" an attorney free of charge.

Review Questions

1. Generally, _____ refers to be economic, educational, or social class that individuals identify with.

2. Social class may be based on culture, _____, age, race, or _____.

3. The _____ class is limited to those with substantial financial resources who exert influence in government and law.

4. The inequities between classes can be _____ or _____ by government policy.

5. The _____ class have little income or property and do not significantly impact law or government.

6. _____ strategies are aimed at decreasing income disparity, which is often linked to criminal behavior.

Critical Thinking Questions

1. Should a public defender being required to spend a predetermined amount of time defending each client, as those who can afford private attorneys would have? Or should the merits of the case dictate how much time the public defender spends on a case?

2. Which crime is more harmful to society, "white-collar" or "street crime"?

3. How does capitalism affect American society?

Chapter 9

Police and the Community: The Significance of this Relationship

August Vollmer, a leading criminal justice professional in the early 20th century said:

> The citizen expects police officers to have the wisdom of Solomon, the courage of David, the strength of Samson, the patience of Job, the leadership of Moses, the kindness of the Good Samaritan, the strategical training of Alexander, the faith of Daniel, the diplomacy of Lincoln, the tolerance of the Carpenter of Nazareth, and finally, an intimate knowledge of every branch of the natural, biological, and social sciences. If he had all these, he might be a good policeman!

Class activities

Identify the role of law enforcement and how they impact our daily lives or others in our communities.

What is a police officer and why are they important to the community? This question is one that reveals expectations of the police but few look into the community relationship until a controversial event is brought to our attention. Law enforcement in the United States is based off of the colonists' English heritage. For centuries, individuals served in a "police" capacity over their families, communities, and regions. Although the concepts of serving and protecting are central to police duties and help to maintain social control, a key component is community involved policing. In both England and colonial America, individuals served as watchmen walking the communities at night to maintain order and alert community members if there was a problem. Depending upon the region some of these individuals were constables or in larger rural areas, sheriffs. Regardless, it was still a partnership with the community. The tradition of limiting government (police) and retaining individual liberty and local police agencies that maintain control have been instrumental in American law enforcement.

The London Metropolitan Police Act of 1829 established a large police force headed by Sir Robert Peel and has served as the foundation for modern law enforcement. Several key components that remain important today are the mission, strategy, and organizational structure. In addition, the police uniform and badge number establish a presence and the authority of an officer, as

© tony4urban/Shutterstock.com

well as providing accountability. Another concept originating in England is the "thin blue line," which symbolizes law enforcement protecting communities from criminals. Throughout history law enforcement priorities and methods shift based on community needs, social issues, and new laws. Currently, we are facing a divide between law enforcement and the communities they serve. Recent events such as officer involved shootings, communication breakdowns, and anti-law enforcement sentiments have contributed to this divide. In some ways, this mirrors issues that have occurred in previous decades, effectively leading to change in policies and methods.

© a katz/Shutterstock.com

Try this

Listen to Paul Harvey-What Are Policemen Made Of?
https://www.youtube.com/watch?v=Dluz-0k3WZA

Law enforcement is different than other professions. A police officer is expected to take charge, solve problems other citizens are incapable of and sometimes become isolated from those not working within the criminal justice system. Police agencies focus on the policies and expectations of the "team" often leaving the individual officer behind in the process. The sudden stress burst, witnessing the best and worst of human nature, and variety of shift hours contribute to the isolation and pressure of the profession.

The U.S. Department of Justice Community Oriented Policing Services identifies the elements of community policing as community partnerships, problem-solving, and organizational transformation. The community partnerships are a key component that emphasizes collaboration to develop trust and solutions to problems in the community. Organizational transformation is another key component where the personnel and data systems are structured to allow for proactive measures to reduce crime and solve problems. The third key component is problem solving. This concept uses the SARA problem solving method (Scanning, Analysis, Response, and Assessment) to look at issues, consider the potential courses of actions, develop a plan, and follow-up with assessing whether it was effective.

The Violent Crime Control and Law Enforcement Act was passed in 1994 and granted communities just under $9 billion to be spent on a variety of initiatives. The intent was to increase the number of police officers who were interacting with community members, to provide training that was more effective to enhance problem-solving opportunities and other skills for working with the community. In addition, the bill was intended to aid in the creation of programs that were unique and allow for community members to work with local, state, or Indian tribal law enforcement agencies to prevent crime within their communities and to create new technology that provided the opportunity for officers to be proactive as opposed to reacting to crime.

The Office of Community Oriented Policing Services was created to determine the allocation of these funds and to monitor the programs initiated through this act. The first phase of the program allowed for the funding of several initiatives focusing on accelerated hiring, education, and employment of police officers.

In 1995, the Universal Hiring Program (UHP) was initiated to fund 100,000 police officers on the streets. Included in that funding was additional training for veterans who were recently hired as part of the Troops to COPS program. In 1995, over $1 billion was spent towards initiatives including the Youth Firearms Violence Initiative. In 1996, more than 52,000 officers were hired through funding from the COPS Office. Almost one and a half billion dollars was spent for hiring the officers, adding the Community Policing to Combat Domestic Violence, Anti-Gang program, and the 311 information program. In 1997, the COPS Office created Regional Community Policing Institutes throughout the nation and focused on several programs such as Advancing Community Policing, Police Integrity Training, and Problem-Solving Partnerships. An additional 75,000 community policing professionals were added throughout the United States in 1998. Other initiatives included focusing on distressed neighborhoods, safe schools, and other school-based partnerships, the Methamphetamine Initiative, and Technology Program were all added for approximately $1.6 billion. The Cops in Schools and Tribal Resources Grant Programs were the focus of 1999 and as of May 1999, the 100,000th community policing officer was funded through the COPS Office. In 2000, the Police as Problem-Solvers and Peacemakers and Justice-Based After School programs were added under the COPS grants and the In-Car Camera program was utilized in 41 state law enforcement agencies.

© Larry Bruce/Shutterstock.com

The terrorist attacks on September 11, 2001 changed American law enforcement forever and provided an opportunity for the COPS Office to support the police agencies responding to the attacks in Pennsylvania, New York, and Virginia. The following years several billion dollars were spent on the Homeland Security Overtime program, Secure Our Schools program, Interoperable Communications Technology program, and Community Policing Development initiative. The events of September 11, 2001 emphasized the issues with police agencies, fire, and medical personnel being unable to communicate directly with each other based on radio technologies that were incompatible.

A 2005 study was commissioned to evaluate whether or not the COPS program was effective. The data demonstrated there were significant declines in crime rates including violent crimes that were attributed to the initiatives sponsored by the COPS Office. The report noted that there was a 15% decrease in crime between 1993 and 2000. The National Community Policing Conference in 2006, Community Policing Leading The Way To A Safer Nation, offered leadership opportunities helping to develop officers' skills on how to implement change, dealing with innovative ideas, integrity and crisis issues, as well as other contemporary issues affecting communities. A milestone was marked in 2007 when the one millionth publication pertaining to the law enforcement field was distributed by the COPS Office. A unique project, the West Side Story Project was introduced. The combination law-enforcement theater program, based on the musical West Side Story, worked with schools and community organizations to help with violence prevention among the youths in the area.

Over the next couple of years funding was used to create the Child Sexual Predator program and after a three-year hiatus the UHP program resumed to add more community policing officers throughout the nation. Recovery Act funding to hire, rehire, or retain approximately 5,000 law enforcement positions and tribal assistance programs were also funded by the COPS Office.

Agencies applying for funding in 2011 were required to identify the public safety problem in their community and provide a plan of how they will use community-policing strategies to resolve this issue. An initiative in 2012 by the COPS Office determined that hiring preference would be given to anyone who is granted an honorable discharge and who served in the military after September 11, 2001. In addition, a collaborative reform review of the Las Vegas Metropolitan Police Department's use of force policies and practices was completed and became a key resource for other police agencies with similar concerns. The focus of 2013 was preference in funding to agencies that were hiring officers who were military veterans, were focusing on building their School Resource Officer program, reducing gun violence and homicide. In addition, $500,000 was awarded to the Virginia Tech Family Outreach Foundation to develop a school safety modeling training curriculum. By year's end, more than 2 million training publications had been distributed through the COPS Office since the inception of the program. The Strengthening the Relationship between Law Enforcement and Communities of Color program kicked off 2014. This program encouraged law enforcement executives, civil rights organizations, and community leaders to work together for problem solving.

Got questions? *(for students)*

For more information on these programs go to http://cops.usdoj.gov/

A part of the community-policing concept is the "Six Pillars of Character" that have been endorsed by the president and the U.S. Senate every year since 1995. The six pillars provide a foundation of six specific ethical values that most people can agree on. Trustworthiness includes being honest not cheating, deceiving, or stealing. Being responsible and reliable following through with what you say you will do. This incorporates doing the right thing even when it requires courage, standing by your loved ones and community and establishing a good reputation. The second pillar of character is respect often referred to as the Golden rule, the concept that is to treat others with respect, accept differences in others, be tolerant and considerate of feelings, use good manners, refrain from hurting anyone, threatening, or hitting and use peaceful means to address anger, disagreements, or insults. The concepts of the responsibility pillar are to persevere, follow through with what you are supposed to do, consider the consequences of your actions before you choose to act, be disciplined and accountable for yourself and be an example for others. The fourth pillar is fairness and includes sharing, being open-minded, treating others fairly and by the rules, not blaming individuals or taking advantage of them. The elements of the fifth pillar are to help people, forgive, show compassion, kindness, and gratitude. The last pillar is citizenship, which represents to get involved with your community, be informed and a good neighbor, respect authority, volunteer, to make your community, whether college, faith, or state a better place.

Law enforcement officers have been a part of many community programs aimed at creating and developing positive relationships with the community. Some of these programs fall directly under Community Oriented Policing units and include a variety of initiatives such as "First Tuesday" where community members come to the local police substation and discuss issues that are affecting their community, crime prevention and safety awareness.

Other COP events are Shop With A Cop, which provides underprivileged children the opportunity to go holiday shopping with police officers (funding is provided) and pick out presents for themselves and their family members. COP units frequently provide gift certificates for holiday meals or deliver entire holiday feasts to the needy within their community. Coffee With A Cop allows citizens to talk one on one with an officer over a cup of coffee.

The youth are an important focus of community policing efforts as the desire to build a positive relationship while a person is young and before they get involved with any criminal activities is believed to be an effective way of building community relations while investing in youth. Several educational programs provide opportunities for police officers to interact with younger members of society. Drug Abuse Resistance Education (DARE), Gang Resistance Education and Training (GREAT), Police Athletic League (PAL), "Every 15 Minutes" and School Resource Officer (SRO) programs allow for youths to interact with law enforcement in a positive setting, learn about law enforcement and issues that may affect youths' lives, play on sports teams coached by officers, and develop character building skills. Police Safety Days provide an opportunity for community members (mostly youths) to observe a variety of demonstrations from specialized police units (K9, SWAT, Search and Rescue, Traffic, and Air support units). Police explorer programs give teens who are interested in a law enforcement career, the chance to develop their knowledge base and skills under the direction of police officers as well as provide community service and leadership opportunities.

Crime prevention efforts are another aspect of working with community partnerships such as Neighborhood Watch programs, services where a crime prevention specialist analyzes safety concerns at a business or residence, and Citizens on Patrol. Citizen's Police Academies are another method of developing community partnerships by providing training over a 12- to 16-week period on various aspects of the police department. This in-depth understanding of the types of services law enforcement provides helps strengthen the relationship and often results in citizens volunteering with the police department.

The relationship between law enforcement and the community will always exist as society entrusts the power to protect and to deprive someone of their liberty to police officers. There are many positive working relationships with various aspects of the community, yet there will remain troubled relationships when police officers are enforcing the laws made by society. Ultimately, developing a relationship remains a collaborative effort with unlimited potential for change and to positively affect everyone's life and community.

Review Questions

1. What key components founded under Sir Robert Peele remain important today in modern policing?

2. According to the text, what events can effect police–community relations?

3. According to the U.S. Department of Justice, what are the elements of community policing?

4. What was the purpose of the UHP?

5. What were law enforcement agencies required to submit in their request for additional funding from COPS?

6. What did the "Law Enforcement and Communities of Color program" that was created in 2014 encourage?

7. What are the "Six Pillars of Character" concepts regarding community policing?

Critical Thinking Questions

1. Which of the "Six Pillars of Character" do you consider most important?

2. How can an effective relationship between a minority community and police ease racial tensions?

3. How did the terrorist attacks on September 11, 2011 change American law enforcement?

4. What are some of the Community Policing Program Initiatives?

Chapter 10

Courts and the Community: Behind the Cloak of Justice

O. J. Simpson, Jodi Arias, and Casey Anthony are names most individuals know. Some of this is based on media coverage, or in O.J.'s case his football career and endorsements prior to 1994. The televised court proceedings for these individuals allowed society to watch the events unfold from the comfort of their living rooms and provided a glimpse, perhaps distorted, of the inner workings of the courtroom. People seldom interact with the court system unless they have been a victim of a crime, received a traffic citation, are a juror, have been arrested or are a loved one of someone who has. With the exception of high school and college students who participate in court initiatives as a way to provide service to the community, interaction with the courts is based on a negative event. Even with cameras in the courtroom, frequent media coverage, and real crime shows, the general public remains unaware of the various partnerships between this segment of the criminal justice system and the community.

Class activities

Discuss as a class the perceptions of what occurs in court, where students obtain information about the courts, and what television shows or movies contribute to this.

The courts encompass the prosecutor, defense attorney, judge, and court personnel. Once an arrest has been made or a case filed with the prosecutor's office to determine whether to pursue charges an individual becomes involved with this part of the criminal justice system. Depending upon the severity of the crime, this relationship may significantly impact someone's life. Prosecutors must look at the evidence and facts of the case to determine if they are likely to be successful in obtaining a conviction before committing the public resources to the case. The inability to prosecute every criminal offense leads to cases with weak evidence to be dropped entirely, to a lower charge, or even extending a plea offer.

The criminal justice system is focused on protecting members of society from others; however, the main focus is on due process. In the criminal courts, the sanctions can range from fines, probation, incarceration, up to the death penalty. An individual who is charged with a crime is provided the opportunity to know what they are being charged with, to have legal counsel provided for them if they cannot afford an attorney, the right to a trial, and the right to confront (cross-examination by defense counsel) witnesses against them. Crime knows no barriers and does not discriminate based on race, gender, or wealth. Despite initiatives to assist crime victims the rights of the accused take precedent since their liberty or life may be taken as a result of a conviction.

Victim advocates

The experiences of victims were not a priority for the criminal justice system for a significant period of time prompting President Ronald Reagan to initiate a task force to identify victim concerns. In 1982, the task force discovered that crime victims were often treated poorly by criminal justice system personnel. The task force provided a report to Congress that recommended a victim be notified of proceedings, be present, and speak during specific proceedings. Although a constitutional amendment was not passed at the federal level, due to the efforts of victims and crime victim specialists, amendments outlining victims' rights were passed in 34 states.

The Victims of Crime Act of 1984 (VOCA) created funding opportunities for various victims services such as advocates, crisis intervention, shelters, and training. Under this act, offenders convicted of Federal crimes are mandated to pay fines on these initiatives. Billions of dollars that are collected from penalties, forfeited bonds, and fines are placed into the Crime Victims Fund once they are collected by the Bureau of Prisons, U.S. Courts and Attorney's Offices. Annually, the funds are dispersed to cover several initiatives starting with child abuse. The first $10 million is used to develop the investigative process and prosecution of these cases. Of the $10 million, Native Americans receive $1.5 million to focus on child abuse and child sexual abuse cases.

The remainder of the funding is divided almost equally between state compensation and assistance programs. All states and U.S. territories received victim assistance funding on an annual basis. There are over 10,000 victims' service organizations that received funding from this act.

The funding is used in a variety of ways including salaries for victim advocates, crisis intervention, counseling, and other areas where victim assistance is needed. Victim advocates may be employed through the prosecutor's office, rape crisis centers, police departments, or domestic violence shelters. Depending upon the organization, the victim advocate duties may differ; however, generally an advocate may respond to a crisis situation, provide emotional support, logistical support such as assisting a domestic violence victim in getting to a shelter, assisting with completing crimes compensation paperwork, transportation to court proceedings, emotional support during the proceedings, and sometimes speaking on behalf of the victim in the court.

Victim advocates employed by the state generally handle crisis interventions for violent crimes such as an attempted murder or murder, work as a liaison between attorneys and victims keeping the victims informed of the case progress, upcoming proceedings, and assisting with recovering property or out-of-pocket expenses. The advocates may be present during an interview with investigators, speak for the victim in court, if they are unable to attend a proceeding or if they are too emotional to speak at a sentencing hearing. Some advocates may work with child victims, while others strictly adults. Advocates may help facilitate a support group such as Survivors of Homicide for the loved ones left behind, or sexual assault and domestic violence support groups. Often victim advocates will conduct "drop charge" seminars when a domestic violence victim is requesting the state drop charges. Although the state is considered the victim of domestic violence, to avoid the numerous issues with the victim initiating the charges, the dynamics of these cases create difficulties with prosecution. Sometimes victims will not show, will lie, or otherwise sabotage the prosecution's efforts on their behalf. For those cases that are generally the first time offense, minor or no injury, or weak evidence, the victim can attend the drop charge seminar where they learn about the dynamics of domestic violence, various phases in an abusive relationship, resources to assist in leaving, and developing an exit strategy. Other assistance may be provided through adopt a phone program where domestic violence or stalking victims are provided a cellular phone free of charge through the district attorney or state attorney's office that only calls 911.

Volunteer programs such as Sexual Assault Victim Services, Court Appointed Special Advocates (CASA), or guardian ad litem train individuals who serve as advocates on a voluntary basis. This may require responding to an emergency room to provide assistance to a sexual assault victim, or work with a neglected or abused child by developing a supportive relationship and making recommendations to the judge who oversees the case. This allows for an independent individual to represent the child's interests as opposed to either parent.

Citizens' academies through the district attorney or state attorney's office provide an opportunity for learning about prosecutor responsibilities, various court proceedings, and specialized courts. For juvenile offenders, two well-known programs are Teen Court and Project Payback. Teen Court is used for nonviolent misdemeanor offenses. In this program, the teen must admit guilt and appears in Teen Court where the sanction is decided. The only adult in the courtroom is a prosecutor who serves in the role of a judge to oversee the proceedings. Other teens, those who may be interested in a career in the criminal justice system or are completing community service through high school programs, serve in the role of the prosecutor, defense attorney, bailiff, and jury members. Since guilt has been admitted each side tries to convince the jury of appropriate sanctions. Ultimately, the jury determines what punishment the defendant will receive. Project Payback allows juvenile offenders who owe restitution to the victim to participate in the program. This provides some life and job skills classes so that a juvenile can obtain employment and repay the victim. In cases where a juvenile is unable to gain employment or too young to work, they can complete community service hours and a stipend of eight dollars for each hour completed is "awarded" to the juvenile's account in order to compensate the victim. Some district attorney offices also have "DA Ambassadors" who speak in schools or at organization meetings to help explain the role of the prosecutor.

Specialized courts

Not all crime is equal. Some offenses traumatize victims while others have little to no impact other than financially. Specialized courts serve a purpose by focusing on the unique characteristics of certain crimes, offenders, or victims. Often this treats the underlying social issues as well as the crime and offender in an effort to reduce recidivism. The prosecutors, public defenders, and judges that serve in these courts receive specialized training pertaining to the issues, victims, and defendants who they work with in order to serve a variety of needs.

Drug courts were some of the first specialized courts where the focus was not just on sanctions for the offender, but also on treatment options. Frequently, the individual is caught up in the cycle of addiction without having rehabilitation opportunities. Domestic violence courts help protect victims due to familiarity with the characteristics of an abusive relationship and an understanding of the dynamics leading to incidents of violence. Mental health courts are more familiar with various psychiatric issues, modes of treatment, inpatient and outpatient resources and other social services that may help treat the defendant, while protecting society and reducing further criminal acts. Veterans Court is a relatively new specialized court that focuses on assisting veterans who are suffering from a variety of issues whether substance or mental health-related. The strategies require familiarity with the pressures veterans returning from deployment often endure that lead to criminal offenses. This holistic approach with specialized courts is beneficial by reducing recidivism, protecting the victim and the community, and assisting the offender in dealing with the underlying issues so they can return to being a productive, law-abiding member of society.

Try this

Research what types of specialty courts are operating within your local area, then compare that to other specialty courts within your state. Is there a need for one type of court more than another?

Review Questions

1. In Teen Court a defendant must _____ before they are allowed to participate.

2. A _____ court focuses on issues related to drug abuse.

3. A _____ court focuses on issues related to mental illnesses.

4. A _____ court focuses on issues related to relationship violence.

5. A _____ court focuses on issues related to mental health, substance abuse and transitioning back to society after serving in combat.

Critical Thinking Questions

1. How are specialty courts beneficial to the community?

2. How has the VOCA 1984 assisted crime victims?

3. What types of services do victim advocates provide?

Chapter 11

Corrections and the Community: Is there a Relationship?

What does the corrections profession have to do with our communities and vice versa? The corrections profession is dealing with those who have been arrested or convicted of a crime how does that impact those of us on the outside?

Class activities

Discuss as a class what role corrections has with the community?

Aside from communication with residents in surrounding areas when there is a crisis, escape from a correctional facility, or mandatory notification for sexual offenders, there is little interaction between the general community and corrections professionals. However, there are aspects of the correctional system that require interaction with the general community, including family members of those who are incarcerated or on probation and parole.

Probation and parole professionals generally have two goals, reducing crime and protecting the community. This is accomplished through a variety of measures such as addressing misconduct and violation of the terms of probation or parole. In addition, probation and parole professionals conduct surveillance and make arrests when appropriate. The indirect assistance this branch of corrections provides to the community is in the measures intended to support the efforts of offenders' to receive appropriate counseling and services in order to become positive, law-abiding community members. This branch of corrections assists both victims and the community with the collection of mandated fees and restitution. The restitution is paid to the victim and is a direct relationship, while the fee collection offsets some of the costs of probation and parole, therefore benefiting all taxpayers.

© f11photo/Shutterstock.com

Correctional facilities have a unique relationship with those who are incarcerated and to a lesser extent the loved ones of the inmates. The majority of the responsibilities of corrections professionals are related to the enforcement of law, policies, and maintaining order

© Joseph Sohm/Shutterstock.com

within facilities. However as intended, there are aspects of the correctional system that are utilized to assist in the rehabilitation of inmates. These programs may differ depending upon the jurisdiction and availability of resources; however, many of them have proven to be beneficial to both the community and those who are incarcerated.

One of the win-win programs operated through the Federal Bureau of Prisons is the Veterans-to-Veterans Service Dog Training Program. This program utilizes incarcerated military veterans to train and nurture service dogs. During the training period, which is seven days a week, instructors from an outside university teach the inmates dog training skills. The dogs and inmates who train them live together in a separate wing of the facility away from other inmates. At the completion of the training, the inmates become certified service dog trainers and the dogs are assigned to veterans in the community who need their services.

Got questions? *(for students)*

Learn more about this program by going to http://www.bop.gov/resources/news/20150327_service_dog_training.jsp

The Federal Bureau of Prisons recognizes the significance of family relationships while an individual is incarcerated and to aid in the reentry process. Several different initiatives are focused on the parent–child relationship, which has proven to benefit the child, the individual, and the community during incarceration and after release.

In New York, the "Mother-Child Night of Hopes and Dreams" provided a unique opportunity for incarcerated women and their families to spend the night together in the prison. This event was focused on the children. Using a larger room at the facility, the staff and community groups decorate it with images and characters popular with children. The children participated in a variety of activities with their mothers such as movies, dancing, games, and crafts. The mothers celebrated the missed birthdays and holidays by putting on an interactive puppet show. The children and mothers read a bedtime story then slept in cots next to one another. For some children, this is the first time in years they have spent the night with their mothers and certainly this was a special night for the mothers who have been away from their children. Another initiative that helps develop constructive relationships is a Mommy and Me Tea held in Connecticut. The incarcerated mothers participate in personal growth classes as well as parenting classes prior to this event. They often create special gifts for their children, which they give at the afternoon tea.

The unique father–daughter relationship benefits both, especially the fathers, when they are reentering society. The fathers are not left out of these initiatives as evidenced with the "There is Still Time at the Ball" event held in Florida. This daddy–daughter dance helps strengthen the relationships prior to the offender's release and increases the likelihood of success as they return to their families and communities. The theme itself is intended to remind the offenders of the opportunity to change and prosper once released.

© Glenn R. McGloughlin/Shutterstock.com

Once an offender is released they are faced with a barrage of issues, where to live, obtaining employment, avoiding the individuals or substances that contributed to their incarceration, and how to pay their bills. Depending upon the skill set an individual had prior to incarceration, skills learned in prison, and the length of incarceration, obtaining employment is often a difficult task. Federal Prison Industries (FPI), also known as UNICOR, is a program that offers educational and vocational training opportunities during incarceration. This wholly-owned government corporation's goal is to provide the inmate with employable skills and assistance in trying to obtain employment on the outside.

Work programs within prisons have been in existence from the late 1700s. These programs are self-sustaining with the profits funding the operational expenses of these programs. Several misconceptions exists pertaining to prison work programs including the belief this is meant to keep prisoners busy, wages are spent on inmate vices, it is a waste of tax dollars, hurts other industries, and is unnecessary.

In reality, recidivism is lowered because prisoners are completing vocational programs through these industries, develop better social skills while participating, and have an increased chance of obtaining employment when they are released. While keeping inmates working helps decrease the disruptions and violence within the prison, the inmates' earnings are used to pay restitution, fines, and child support. UNICOR does not require public funding and obtains their supplies, equipment, and materials from small businesses. Often these businesses are owned by minorities or the disadvantaged. In this capacity, UNICOR supports local businesses because the products do not generally go to the community, only the government and limits its advertising. In addition the real product from UNICOR is an inmate who develops skills and experience, then returns to the community as a productive citizen. The program is necessary to help inmates develop skills, work habits, pay restitution and fines, and most importantly find employment once released and reduce recidivism.

Try this

Go to this website and check out the many products created in our prisons. http://www.unicor.gov/shopping/viewcat_m.asp?iStore=UNI

Many prison systems focus on an inmate's release almost immediately upon entry into the system. This focus intensifies closer to the release date when inmates are offered educational programs intended to help with gaining and maintaining employment, basic clothing and transportation needs, as well as readjusting to society. The Federal Bureau of Prisons utilizes the Release Preparation Program, Inmate Transition Branch, and Residential Reentry Centers to assist in the transition. The Inmate Transition Branch assists inmates in gathering their resumes, transcripts, and educational certificates to apply to posted positions. In addition, mock job fairs and interviews allow inmates to practice their interview skills and introduce recruiters to the inmates.

Another aspect of corrections working with the community is with victim/witness notification. These initiatives are known by different names depending upon the state or federal level; however, the intent is the same, keeping victims and witnesses informed about crucial events, such as a prisoner release or a hearing.

Got questions? *(for students)*

http://www.bop.gov/resources/victim_resources.jsp and for the state of Nevada http://www.doc.nv.gov/node/75

Reintegrating into society after incarceration is difficult for both the inmates and their families. Community-based partnerships strive to make this transition easier and successful. One such program is called Hope for Prisoners. This is in the Las Vegas area and helps former inmates seek employment and work with mentors who are often volunteer police officers. This provides an opportunity to interact with officers in a different capacity and provides skills to adjust to society and maintain a crime free life.

Review Questions

1. What is the Veterans-to-Veterans Service Dog Training Program?

2. What is UNICOR?

3. What types of parent-child events does the Federal Bureau of Prisons offer?

Critical Thinking Questions

1. What are the benefits of children participating in activities with their parents inside correctional facilities? How does this help the offender, child, and community?

2. What are the benefits to prisoners working while incarcerated?

3. What types of assistance do reentry programs give the incarcerated?

Chapter 12

Reverse Discrimination and the Vilification of White Males

The concept for this chapter is based on classroom experience while facilitating a community relations class. Previously when teaching community relations our department required a textbook that did not provide the perspectives of criminal justice professionals and was heavily biased against white males. Several classes included less than three white males in a room full of approximately 35 students. Although this is not the norm, this provided a unique learning opportunity for everyone. As the course progressed and various transgressions against groups of minorities were detailed in the text and class discussions, there were awkward moments. Most of it centered around the white males when acts of discrimination over the last few centuries were discussed. Although there was no outward hostility, it was clear the white males recognized they were viewed differently and were the minority in the class. The interaction was fascinating considering the classroom environment did not provide an opportunity for overt hostility or discrimination.

Many segments of society have been the victim of discriminatory acts based on their gender, race, religion, or ethnicity. History books are filled with transgressions, case law and constitutional amendments validate the existence of these acts, and one only has to turn on

© Rob Wilson/Shutterstock.com

any form of media today to witness the perceptions of continued acts of discrimination. The focus is seldom on bias within genders, races, or religions, but on vilifying the white male. Although as a society we proclaim values judging one based on their actions as opposed to the color of their skin, their gender, or religion, when it comes to a white male, these values are often forgotten. Reverse discrimination is a term to describe when members of the historically advantaged and majority group are discriminated against.

Ironically, the Civil Rights Act of 1964 has served as the basis for reverse discrimination complaints, as early as 1976. In 1970, three employees of the Santa Fe Trail Transportation Company were jointly charged due to misappropriating approximately 60 gallons of antifreeze from a shipment. Two of the three employees were terminated while the third, an African American male was retained. The two white employees filed a discrimination suit. Although the judicial process was lengthy, eventually the Supreme Court weighed in on the case (*McDonald et al. v. Santa Fe Trail Transportation Company 1976*). The Court considered that a reversal of the situation with a black plaintiff would result in discrimination therefore McDonald and Laird, his co-plaintiffs as white males were the victims of discrimination that are clearly outlined in statute. The Court interpreted legislation as applicable to all persons regardless of race or color.

Got questions? *(for students)*

Want to learn more about civil rights? Go to http://www.justice.gov/crt/

A consent decree is part of a court order that specifies actions one of the parties in the case must cease or begin. The consent decree is often preferred in cases where the defendant wants to avoid exposure and the plaintiff desires accountability. In 1987, a group of African American police officers settled on a consent decree with the City of New Orleans. For 14 years, the group had been in litigation over alleged discriminatory policies for promotion and hiring. As a result of the consent decree, a new hiring and promotion system was instituted to remedy racial discrimination that had previously occurred. As part of this agreement, the City of New Orleans was mandated to finance almost 45 additional positions strictly for African-American officers. Two of these openings were for captains, 12 for lieutenants and 30 sergeants. In addition, the promotional process was changed to eliminate individual rankings on promotional lists and instead establish a grouping system that consolidated individuals of similar rankings. In 1994, a group of 24 officers who were not African-American pursued legal action for reverse discrimination when they were not promoted. The final determination was that city had violated the equal protection clause of the 14th Amendment when it failed to promote officers who were not African-American.

© John Roman Images/Shutterstock.com

The Flint Police Department (Michigan) created a temporary quota system for promotion to sergeant as a result of a consent decree in the 1970s. During the next two decades, a variety of decisions intended to increase the number of minorities in the police department led to various claims of reverse discrimination. In 2011, a group of 48 officers were awarded almost $4 million as a result of reverse discrimination. The officers filed their case after the mayor ignored promotional procedures in 2006 and a white female and four African American men were promoted to an elite unit, completely bypassing the white males.

Despite this award in 2011 and 2012, the leadership of the Flint Police Department circumvented promotional procedures once again in favor of minorities. In this instance, they created provisional promotions, and then later tested individuals who were serving in those positions to determine if they were eligible to remain. Despite several African American employees failing the exam, they were allowed to remain in their positions. A group of 14 officers filed a lawsuit based on these acts and retaliation. This case is currently pending.

In 2014, Christopher Barrella, a white male police lieutenant was awarded $1.35 million, including punitive damages, as a result of discrimination based on his race. Lieutenant Barrella had completed the Civil Service Chief of Police Exam in the number one spot. The Village of Freeport Police Department, New York, did not promote Barrella, and instead a Hispanic male was promoted to chief although he had scored lower on the exam than other white applicants.

The success of these lawsuits demonstrates that anyone can be a victim of discrimination. Although many of the actions that formed the basis of these cases were intended to remedy past, they did so by discriminating against others. This demonstrates the difficulties in creating qualified, diverse workforces while balancing the rights of all individuals.

Review Questions

1. What is reverse discrimination?

2. What is a consent decree?

Critical Thinking Question

How does an organization effectively remedy wrongs of the past without discriminating against other groups?

Bibliography

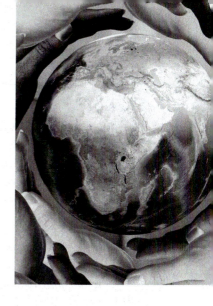

19th Amendment to the U.S. Constitution: Women's Right to Vote (1920). (n.d.). Retrieved from http://www.ourdocuments.gov/doc.php?flash=true&doc=63

A short history of Asians in America. (2007, September). [Video file]. Available from: *http://www. youtube.com/watch?v=6hVlSuuaQhs*

America seen through the eyes of an illegal immigrant – documentary. (2011, April). [Video file]. Available from: *https://www.youtube.com/watch?v=v_UTYLWfqWs*

American Bar Association. (n.d.). *Model rules of professional conduct*. Retrieved from: http://www. americanbar.org/groups/professional_responsibility/publications/model_rules_of_professional_conduct.html

American Holocaust of Native American Indians. (2011, November). [Video file]. Available from: *https://www.youtube.com/watch?v=gTrbVf6SrCc*

Beck, A., & Karberg, J. C. (2001). Prison and jail inmates at midyear 2000. Bureau of Justice Statistics Retrieved from: http://www.bjs.gov/index.cfm?ty=dcdetail&iid=245

BrainyQuote. (n.d.). Martin Luther King, Jr. Retrieved from http://www.brainyquote.com/quotes/quotes/m/martinluth133707.html

Bureau of Justice Statistics (2013). Criminal Victimization 2013. Retrieved from: http://www.bjs.gov/index.cfm?ty=pbdetail&iid=5113

Carson, A. & Sabol, W. (2012). *Prisoners in 2011*. Washington, DC: Bureau of Justice Statistics.

Centers for Disease Control. (2013). Mental illness. Retrieved from: http://www.cdc.gov/mentalhealth/basics/mental-illness.htm

Centers for Disease Control. (2013). *Mental illness surveillance among U.S. adults*. Retrieved from: http://www.cdc.gov/mentalhealthsurveillance/

Clark County CASA Program. (2013). Court Appointed Special Advocate. Retrieved from: http://www.casalasvegas.org/become-a-casa/

Clark County District Attorney's Office. (n.d.). The criminal division. Retrieved from: http://www.clarkcountynv.gov/depts/district_attorney/crm/Pages/default.aspx

Class structure in the U.S. (2015). Boundless Sociology. Retrieved from: https://www.boundless.com/sociology/textbooks/boundless-sociology-textbook/stratification-inequality-and-social-class-in-the-u-s-9/the-class-structure-in-the-u-s-75/class-structure-in-the-u-s-442-10206/

Coolican, J. P. (2013, march 7). The tragedy of Stanley Gibson's death began days before he was shot by police. Retrieved from: http://lasvegassun.com/news/2013/mar/07/tragedy-stanley-gibsons-death-actually-began-days-/

Coston, B. & Kimmel, M. (2013). White men as the new victims: Reverse discrimination cases and the men's rights movement. *Nevada Law Journal* 13(29), 368–385.

Crossing the line: Border stories. (2010, July). [Video file]. Available from: http://www.youtube.com/watch?v=1PaWiYOH8O0

Danilina, S. (n.d.) *Who was Myra Bradwell: America's first woman lawyer.* Retrieved from: http://thelawdictionary.org/article/who-was-myra-bradwell-americas-first-woman-lawyer/

Difference. (n.d.). In *Merriam-Webster dictionary online.* Retrieved from http://www.merriam-webster.com/dictionary/difference

Differences between men's and women's prisons. (n.d.). Retrieved from: http://education-portal.com/academy/lesson/differences-between-mens-womens-prisons.html

Domestic violence accounted for about a fifth of all violent victimizations between 2003 and 2012. (2014, April). Retrieved from: http://www.bjs.gov/content/pub/press/ndv0312pr.cfm

Elliot, J. (2013, November). *Brown eyes and blue eyes experiment* [Video file]. Available from: *http://www.youtube.com/watch?v=-Ggq7XfYl58*

Ethnicity v. Race. (n.d.). Diffen. Retrieved from: http://www.diffen.com/difference/Ethnicity_vs_Race

Federal Bureau of Investigation. (2010). *About hate crime statistics.* Retrieved from: https://www.fbi.gov/about-us/cjis/ucr/hate-crime/2010/resources/hate-crime-2010-about-hate-crime

Federal Bureau of Investigation. (2013). *National Incident Based Reporting System.* Retrieved from: https://www.fbi.gov/about-us/cjis/ucr/nibrs/2013

Federal Bureau of Investigation. (2013). *Uniform Crime Report.* Retrieved from: https://www.fbi.gov/about-us/cjis/ucr/crime-in-the-u.s/2013/crime-in-the-u.s.-2013/violent-crime/violent-crime-topic-page/violentcrimemain_final

Federal Bureau of Prisons. (n.d.) Resources. Retrieved from: http://www.bop.gov/resources/

Gang Resistance Education And Training (n.d.). Office of Juvenile Justice and Delinquency Prevention. Retrieved from: https://www.great-online.org/GREAT-Home

Goodreads (n.d.). Sri Aurobindo. Retrieved from http://www.goodreads.com/author/quotes/5867530.Sri_Aurobindo

Guerino, P., Harrison, P. M., & Sabol, W. (2011). *Prisoners in 2010.* Bureau of Justice Statistics. Retrieved from: http://www.bjs.gov/index.cfm?ty=dcdetail&iid=245

Harvey, P. (2013, February). *What are policemen made of?* [Video file]. Available from: https://www.youtube.com/watch?v=Dluz-0k3WZA

History. (n.d.). John Locke. Retrieved from http://www.history.com/topics/john-locke

Homicide in the U.S. Known to Law Enforcement, 2011 (2013, December). Retrieved from: http://www.bjs.gov/content/pub/pdf/hus11.pdf

Justia U.S. Supreme Court. (n.d.). Barrella v. Village of Freeport et al. Retrieved from: http://law.justia.com/cases/federal/district-courts/new-york/nyedce/2:2012cv00348/326540/30/

Justia U.S. Supreme Court. (n.d.). Craig v. Boren, 429 U.S. 190 (1976). Retrieved from: https://supreme.justia.com/cases/federal/us/429/190/case.html

Las Vegas Metropolitan Police Department. (2015). *Community Programs.* Retrieved from: http://www.lvmpd.com/

Las Vegas Metropolitan Police Department. (2015). *Crisis Intervention Team.* Retrieved from: http://www.lvmpd.com/

Mallory, C. & Sears, B. (2014, July). Discrimination against state and local government LGBT employees: An analysis of administrative complaints. Retrieved from: http://williamsinstitute.law.ucla.edu/?s=Sexual+Orientation+Law+and+Public+Policy+&cat=3

National Alliance on Mental Illness. (2013). Mental health conditions. Retrieved from: http://www.nami.org/Learn-More/Mental-Health-Conditions

National Archives and Records Administration. (n.d.). *The charters of freedom.* Retrieved from http://www.archives.gov/exhibits/charters/constitution_transcript.html

National Institute of Justice (n.d.). Specialized courts. Retrieved from: http://www.nij.gov/topics/courts/pages/specialized-courts.aspx

National's Women Law Center (n.d.). Reed v. Reed at 40: A Landmark Decision. Retrieved from: http://www.nwlc.org/resource/reed-v-reed-40-landmark-decision

Nearly 100 union backers arrested in protest of Cosmopolitan. (2013, March). [Video file]. Available from: http://www.vegasinc.com/business/2013/mar/D

Poverty guidelines. (2015). Federal Register (80)14. Retrieved from: http://www.gpo.gov/

Rape, Abuse, and Incest National Network. (2015). How often does sexual assault occur? Retrieved from: https://rainn.org/get-information/statistics/frequency-of-sexual-assault

Ridley, G. (2014, July 14). *Federal appeals court allows Flint cops' racial discrimination lawsuit to move forward.* Retrieved from: http://www.mlive.com/news/flint/index.ssf/2014/07/federal_appeals_court_allows_f.html

Riots, bullets, tear gas in Ferguson. (2014, November). [Video file]. Available from: *http://www.cnn.com/videos/bestoftv/2014/11/25/orig-raw-scenes-from-ferguson-npr.cnn*

Sawabona Association. (n.d.). Sawabona story. Retrieved from http://sawabonaassociation.com/home/

Siegel, L. S. (2015). *Criminology* (5th edition). Stamford: Cengage Learning.

Six Pillars of Character (n.d.) Josephson Institute.Retrieved from: https://charactercounts.org/sixpillars.html

Stonewall forty years later. (2009, June). [Video file]. Available from: *http://www.youtube.com/watch?v=mTujTI8rGBg*

Teen Court. (2015). State Attorney's Office Eighteenth Judicial Circuit. Retrieved from http://www.sa18.state.fl.us/page/teen-court-peer-court.html.

The Criminology and Criminal Justice Collective of Northern Arizona University. (2008). *Investigating difference: Human and cultural relations in criminal justice* (2nd Edition). Upper Saddle River, New Jersey: Prentice Hall.

The rise and fall of Jim Crow. (2009, October). [Video file]. Available from: http://www.youtube.com/watch?v=ChWXyeUTKg8

The sentencing project (2012). Incarcerated Women. Retrieved from: http://www.sentencingproject.org/doc/publications/cc_incarcerated_women_factsheet_sep24sp.pdf

The Victims of Crime Act of 1984 (VOCA). (n.d.). Offices of the United States Attorneys. Retrieved from: http://www.justice.gov/usao/priority-areas/victims-rights-services/victims-rights

Trial by peers. (2014). Clark County Law Foundation. Retrieved from https://www.clarkcountybar.org/resources/clark-county-law-foundation/

UNICOR. (n.d.) Factories with fences: The history of UNICOR. Retrieved from: http://www.unicor.gov/shopping/viewcat_m.asp?iStore=UNI

U. S. Census. (2015). *Population estimates.* Retrieved from: http://www.census.gov/popest/data/index.html

U. S. Census. (n.d.). *What we do.* Retrieved from http://www.census.gov/about/what.html

U. S. Department of Justice. (n.d.). Civil Rights Division. Retrieved from: http://www.justice.gov/crt/

U. S. Department of Justice (n.d.). *Victims of Crime Act crime victims fund.* Retrieved from: https://www.ncjrs.gov/ovc_archives/factsheets/cvfvca.htm

U.S. Department of Justice Community Oriented Policing Services. (2015). 20 years of community policing. Retrieved from: http://www.cops.usdoj.gov/

United States House of Representatives. (n.d.). *The legislative process.* Retrieved from: http://www.house.gov/content/learn/legislative_process/

Walker, S. & Katz. C. (2012). The police in America: An introduction (8th Edition). New York, NY:McGraw-Hill Education.

White, M. & Escobar, G. (2008) Making good cops in the Twenty-First Century: Emerging issues for the effective recruitment, selection, and training of police in the United States and abroad," *International Review of Law, Computers, and Technology Crime and Criminal Justice* 22(1–2), 119–134.

Women professionals in corrections: A growing asset. (2008). Retrieved from: http://www.mtctrains.com/sites/default/files/WomenProfessionalsInCorrections-Aug08.pdf

CPSIA information can be obtained
at www.ICGtesting.com
Printed in the USA
LVOW01s0418021216

515051LV00004B/12/P